Praise for *Maggie*

Anyone looking for meaning in the face of tragedy will treasure *Maggie Lee for Good*. This beautifully written and heartfelt account of parents dealing with their child's premature death will provide hope and inspiration for all who read it.

—Travis Stork, MD
Host of the Emmy™-award winning TV show *The Doctors*

Jinny Henson is my friend. Her quick wit and talent is just the formula to be a great comedian. And then horrific tragedy struck her life. I watched her tread through the deep waters of grief—the place mothers fear most in this world. In this book, Jinny and John have allowed us to peer into the most intimate places in their hearts—their pain. We can all see that crying and laughing are tenderly linked and that God can amazingly use both to draw us closer and closer to Him. Thank you for taking us along.

—Chonda Pierce
"Queen of Clean Comedy," best selling author and
performer, TV and radio personality

With this book Jinny and John Henson bravely report from the depths of a place all of us hope never to visit—grief from the loss of a child. For anyone coping with loss or doubting their faith, reading *Maggie Lee for Good* proves that even from the darkest places something positive can emerge, and that we can lose something we love even more than our own life, and somehow find a way to keep living.

—Christie Taylor Seaver
Former editor, *Cara*, the Aer Lingus magazine
Freelance writer for the *Sunday Times* and *The Irish Times*

Jinny and John Henson have "done good" by the life and memory of their daughter, Maggie Lee. This is a brave, faithful, and generous book about a precious and loving girl, the pain of her passing, and the grace and redemption inspired by her faithful life.

—Marv Knox
Editor of *The Baptist Standard*

Smyth & Helwys Publishing, Inc.
6316 Peake Road
Macon, Georgia 31210-3960
1-800-747-3016
©2012 by John and Jinny Henson
All rights reserved.
Printed in the United States of America.

The paper used in this publication meets the minimum requirements of
American National Standard for Information Sciences—
Permanence of Paper for Printed Library Materials.
ANSI Z39.48–1984. (alk. paper)

Library of Congress Cataloging-in-Publication Data

CIP Information on file

MAGGIE LEE
FOR GOOD

JINNY AND JOHN HENSON

Dedicated to our son, Jack,
whose strength, humor, and faith inspire us

And to the Alabama National Guard troops
for their bravery on July 12, 2009

Contents

Acknowledgments

Without the enthusiastic participation of thousands of friends and strangers in Maggie Lee for Good Day each October 29th, there would be no book by this name. We stand in awe of God, who is in the business of creative redemption and of those who faithfully follow His leading, even to give a pony tail, cook a meal, or drill a water well in Malawi. This book is our thank you note as well as a glimpse from our vantage point of supreme gratitude.

We appreciate those of you who read our blogs and CaringBridge posts and kept asking, "So, when is the book coming out?" You were probably joking, but we took you seriously. Particular thanks go to Mimi, whose gentle "encouragement" to finish the book never waned.

To Dr. Olivia Holloway McIntyre, who graciously slogged through our first written efforts with grace, even at times via iPhone from rural locations, we say thanks. Your intellect and vision shaped this manuscript in significant ways. Aunt Holly, you are indeed the Honey Badger of editing.

We are indebted to Jay Greenleaf and Michael Siegel for the well-informed input on this project. We miss you profoundly, Jay, and your legacy of unmerited grace to the downtrodden continues to inspire us to serve Christ with greater sacrifice each day.

To our favorite authors: Frederick Buechner, Thomas Merton, N. T. Wright, St. John of the Cross, Anne Lamott, John Claypool, and Gerald Sittser. Your books have been lifelong friends and inspirations to us especially as we approached the daunting task of writing our own.

We acknowledge the strength of our families and faithful friends who stepped into our pain when it was too great for us to bear alone then readily jumped into a project to honor Maggie Lee. We will never forget her, but, thanks to you, we never have to remember her alone. Your relentless prayers that continue to this day have sustained us and made this story possible.

This book was written in the midst of planting Church for the Highlands. After losing our child—when we did not know for certain if we had a church plant in us—graciously you believed we did. We are thankful to our Church for the Highlands family for your vision to bring heaven to earth with your acts of kindness to the least of these. The blessing of co-laboring with you in this counter-culture ministry experiment has enriched our lives. The way you seek to serve rather than be served is a rare and beautiful thing to watch. The Kingdom of God is a party and what diverse, festive invitations you are.

We are grateful for the skillful editing of Leslie Andres, cover design of Daniel Emerson, and book design and graphics of Dave Jones of Smyth & Helwys. Thank you for making this project something far more than we ever could on our own.

To Eric Sorenson, Shreveport photographer who captured the picture of Maggie Lee and Ellie, and to Erin Anderson, photographer and graphic artist in Houston who designed the MLFG logo, we thank you.

Lastly, we acknowledge Maggie Lee. As she struggled for and ultimately lost her earthly life, stories of her unique faith emerged. These stories of her standing up for the weak and helping the least of these inspired others to do the same. Although the tragedy of her premature death and the projects people have adopted in her name may paint her as a superhero, she did not leap over tall buildings with a single bound or have X-ray vision. Her handwriting was messy, and her laugh was at times far too loud. She was, however, a young lady with practical faith, true Christ-like compassion, and love for justice. Funny, exuberant, talented, imperfect, and inspired, she inspired us. For good.

When your heart is breaking,
Don't eat Ben & Jerry's.
When you feel like quitting,
No 'nanna puddin'.
When you're feelin' bad or sad,
Lay your worries on God.
      —Maggie Lee Henson, 2008 (11 years old)

Jinny and John Henson
Shreveport, Louisiana

Chapter 1

"Mommy, Am I Going to Die?"

"Mommy, am I going to die?" my terrified twelve-year-old daughter asked one January night. It cut through the thick fog of Vicks VapoRub and immediately pierced my heart.

Maggie Lee had struggled since October with a mysterious illness that blood tests and even a CT scan failed to diagnose. Finally after a specific test for the mycoplasma organism, we had our answer. Weeks later, Maggie Lee's residual cough left us just as perplexed as we were before.

After Christmas when her health did not improve appreciably, our pediatrician sent us to a pulmonologist, whose concern for the level of obstruction in Maggie Lee's airway led her to order a bronchoscopy. The upcoming procedure was the impetus behind Maggie Lee's dramatic question.

She had the bronchoscopy and, fortunately, cancer was ruled out. Since my mother-in-law and father had died of cancer, I naturally feared that a tumor might be obstructing my daughter's airway. I was thoroughly relieved by the results and felt that God knew I could never handle having a child with such a horrific illness.

Maggie Lee's health turned the corner almost immediately after the test. She even insisted on going to the Mardi Gras Ball at St. Joseph School in Shreveport the night of the procedure. With newfound health, she spent the spring of her sixth grade year preparing for a show choir performance, out-of-town birthday parties, and her annual appearance in her school talent show.

A natural performer, Maggie Lee was prone to bellow Taylor Swift's songs or the sound track from the musical *Wicked* from her second floor "Broadway"-themed bedroom—a bedroom whose proximity to the stairwell ensured that her voice resonated to every nook and cranny of our 1923 Dutch Colonial home.

Musical theater was her dream, but her goals, as self-recorded on her flip video camera, included being a better singer, being a better actor, being a better daughter, and being a better Christian.

With confidence and humility, Maggie Lee moved through life expressing her faith in unpredictable ways. She cared about homeless people and, when we happened to see someone with a sign asking for money for food, she asked if we could get them a hamburger. She noticed marginalized classmates and included them at her lunch table. She even gave "mean lessons"—more like boundary lessons—to a girl in her class who was being taken advantage of by another sixth-grade girl. Maggie Lee hated to see injustice in any form and was quick to try to make things right.

Her school locker was cluttered, but her purpose was clear. As Shreveport Mayor Cedric Glover said in 2011 when he proclaimed October 29, "Maggie Lee for Good Day," "Maggie Lee understood her purpose, and that purpose was to touch the lives of others and serve them in ways that she could." Indeed it was. She lived and loved with reckless abandon, and when tragedy fell, stories of her unique brand of faith spread.

Maggie Lee sparkled from the inside, and now we are left to settle for her sparkling from inside of us rather than bellowing show tunes from the top of the stairs. The story that remains is one part worst-case scenario and three parts God's creative redemption, a beautiful tale we wished we were merely reading rather than writing.

"No, honey, you are not going to die! You are going to be just fine," I told Maggie Lee that January night. How could I have known that in just seven months, a tragic accident would make that reassuring statement a hideous lie?

Chapter 2

July 12, 2009

When I was in seminary, I began to share the good news of God's grace through humor as a Christian comedian. I took six years off to have my children and then, without missing a beat, God began opening doors for me to perform for churches again when Maggie Lee was a first grader. Sometimes speaking engagements took me out of town, but thanks to the miracle of unlimited data plans, my daughter and I were in perpetual communication.

Although Maggie Lee had me listed as "BFF" (best friends forever) in the address book of her phone, as she approached teenage years, I knew I was growing dorkier at a feverish pace. I have to believe that had she lived, she would most likely consider me a leper at this point. Notwithstanding my plummeting status, we were in constant contact. From the time my husband, John, our son, Jack, and Maggie Lee dropped me off at the Shreveport Regional Airport until I touched back down, we would text.

Whether it was telling me how skinny I was getting (oh, the optimism) or encouraging me in my hospice marketing job, Maggie Lee was as much a cheerleader for me as my closest friends were. She was how I imagined a sister might be.

I vividly remember her encouragement one snowy spring night in 2009 in Kearney, Nebraska, before I performed. I mentally reviewed my set list and prayed that my Southern humor would somehow translate into "Cornhusker." It was cold in the makeshift greenroom of the geodesic church, but my daughter's words warmed me. She text-messaged that she had prayed for me and that I would do great. Her prayers worked. Similarly, she encouraged John, her "Dada," as she called him, before he preached on Sundays as associate pastor at First Baptist Church Shreveport.

On Saturday, July 11, 2009, my performance jitters were history as the Women's Retreat at Woodlawn United Methodist Church in Panama City Beach, Florida, came to a close. I hit the beach and spent about an hour on the phone talking to the kids. The next day, I went to church with my host, Nancy Dennis, who was one of my mother's best childhood friends from Jackson, Mississippi. After the early service at Woodlawn and part of Sunday school, we left to get to the airport in plenty of time for my connecting flights to Memphis and then, ultimately, Shreveport.

Earlier that morning, Maggie Lee's youth group had departed for Passport Camp in Macon, Georgia. Along with offering typical Christian summer camp activities (swimming, team-building, speakers), Passport focused on mission projects during the day with worship and activities at night. Maggie Lee was especially excited about a trip to the water park on the way back to Shreveport after Passport.

The First Baptist Church of Shreveport bus was loaded with luggage, youth, and sponsors. The youth minister, Jason, asked my husband John, the associate pastor, to pray for the trip. John prayed for safe travels and God's protection, and he and our ten-year-old son, Jack, drove the few blocks home while the bus headed east on I-20.

Had Nancy and I not left Sunday school early that morning, I would have missed a phone call with Maggie Lee. As we got into Nancy's car, I turned on my phone and up popped numerous texts from my daughter. They primarily focused on when the first pit stop would be. I decided to call her. The background bus hum was typical youth frivolity powered by sleep deprivation and sugar. Maggie Lee told me that they had stopped at McDonald's and asked me how I was. We chatted for a few brief moments, and then we said good-bye. I ended with "I love you, honey." "Love you, too, Mama," she responded. That was shortly after 10:00 a.m.

At the Panama City Beach airport, Nancy dropped me off curbside for my departing flight. With only carry-on luggage, I headed directly to security, preparing to remove my jacket and shoes and any other potentially dangerous items. As I began to shove my Blackberry cell phone into an overstuffed purse, it lit up. I looked at the text from my friend, Doneen: "church bus flipped." Shocked, I backed out of security and redialed Maggie Lee's number—the number I had used not ten minutes earlier. I called over and over then tried the number for everyone I knew who was on the trip.

Finally, a voice on the other end told me, "There were four children taken by stretcher to the hospital, and Maggie Lee was one of them. I'm so sorry." The terrified voice cracked and I could hear sirens and crying in the background. My greatest fears were confirmed; I had to reach my daughter somehow. My flight, scheduled to leave in ninety minutes, was to Memphis. Though I had no idea if it would be quicker to drive to Meridian, Mississippi, from Panama City or to wait an hour and a half, fly to Memphis, and then drive to Meridian, I knew there was no way I could sit still. Sobbing prayers, I rented a car and set off to get to my daughter.

In Shreveport, John was stepping into the pulpit to preach when he heard the news. He and Jack went home, threw clothes into a bag, and headed for the Shreveport airport. A family in the church had offered the use of their plane to get parents to their injured children in Meridian, Mississippi. Others immediately came forward to help, like Francis, who secured our other two dogs and took them to a friend's house.

John and I talked, and he asked if he should bring Ellie, Maggie Lee's Chihuahua. I told him that I thought the dog would cheer up Maggie Lee in rehab. At that point, I had no idea how grave her injuries were. We soon learned that both Maggie Lee and another girl, Lauren, had been flown to Batson Children's Hospital at the University Medical Center in Jackson, Mississippi. Both of the girls, along with Brandon, a fourteen-year-old boy, were ejected from the bus when it flipped.

Details came in sketchy spurts as I frantically drove. I had never heard of a bus flipping before and was overwhelmed by the thought of that huge vehicle coming to rest on Lauren and Maggie Lee. Miraculously, an Alabama National Guard Troop that had left training exercises early that Sunday morning had witnessed the entire accident. The day before, they had undergone training in how to upright overturned vehicles, which they did immediately for the flipped bus. Their heroic action and their prayers that day helped many of our children.

I discovered that the problem with having a tragedy on Sunday morning is that my family was all in church. Fortunately, my Catholic brother, Brink, goes to Mass on Saturday evening and was accessible by phone. I asked him to be there when my mother got home from Westbury Baptist. He was extremely broken up and immediately began to pray.

One by one, I called my family members and tried my best to field calls as I made my way through Florida's Panhandle. I spoke with John again, and he told me that Maggie Lee and Lauren had been flown via helicopter to Jackson, Mississippi, and he would be there soon. Well, I thought, surely there was still hope if she was being transported by helicopter. Maggie Lee's friend, Sara, had also been injured and would eventually wind up at University Medical Center as well. Some of the youth and sponsors suffered broken bones and serious lacerations. Others had minor injuries.

Just as we hung up, I answered a call from the ER doctor from the Meridian Hospital where Maggie Lee was originally taken. She asked me where I was, and I told her that I was driving to Jackson. She asked if anyone was with me and advised me to pull over, which I was not about to do. In my shock, I searched my scattered mind to come up with a question I would later regret not asking. In the stream of misinformation, I had originally heard that Maggie Lee had been responsive, but this ER doctor put that rumor to rest. "No, she never responded."

I found it absurd to talk to a doctor about my unresponsive daughter who had been thrown from a bus on the way to youth camp. The story became more surreal by the moment. I repeatedly shouted out to God, begging him through sobs to save our daughter as I drove in numbness.

My friend, Jenny, in Pensacola Beach called and told me that I could not drive at a time like this. She insisted on driving me to Meridian. I reluctantly agreed. She met me along I-10 and took over while I fielded phone call after phone call. John was now in Jackson and relayed the grave news that Brandon was pronounced dead.

Tammy, who had volunteered her airplane, called to coordinate a location where the pilot who dropped off parents in Jackson and Meridian could meet me and fly me to Jackson. After several phone calls, she told us to head to Hattiesburg, Mississippi, where the private plane would meet us.

While I was en route to the airstrip, John called to tell me that the pediatric neurosurgeon at Batson Children's was set to do a craniotomy as soon as Maggie Lee could be stabilized. In this procedure, a flap of the skull is removed to allow the brain to swell and reduce intracranial pressure. Just as I was boarding the small plane in Hattiesburg, John called with awful news. "Her heart has stopped three times," he said. "They can't do the surgery to relieve the swelling. They say to hurry."

With that pronouncement came an even deeper level of unreality. I had this strange sense of being supported; I knew that no matter what happened, we would be okay. That Maggie Lee might not be okay, but we would. I knew that my daughter could be dead before the thirty-minute flight to Jackson was over. I knew that I might never get to say a last good-bye to her. I also knew undoubtedly that in this worst-case scenario, God was literally carrying me.

John updated me every few minutes. The plane landed, and one of John's old friends from his days at Camp Ridgecrest drove me to Batson Children's Hospital at University Medical Center. I tore through the entry, up the elevator, and into the Pediatric Intensive Care waiting room where those who had gotten there before me fell silent. I was buzzed in by the nurse and sprinted to the left side of the PICU. A team of people in light-blue scrubs scurried around my child, who was connected to more tubes than I could count.

I saw John. He looked strong but terrified, and he embraced me. Then I saw Maggie Lee's face. She was beautiful. Even with tape around her nose and a patch of hair shaved from the very top of her crown, she was ravishing. I tried to grab her foot as the medical team scurried around. There was no way to get to her for the embrace I longed to give, even though I knew it would only be one-sided. With her heart somewhat stabilized, the doctor pulled me aside, explaining that they could not do the surgery because her heart had stopped.

Even though they had revived her, Maggie Lee most likely would not make it through the night.

"I understand, but there are already thousands of people praying for her," I insisted. I was well aware of the obvious severity of her injuries but had to leave room for God to work. The doctor explained the gravity of her brain injuries, how her lung was punctured, and that her heart was trying to stop. I took it all in and thanked him for caring for our child. He let out a labored sigh as a tear welled up behind his glasses. I didn't know much about ICU doctors, but I knew that they are trained not to cry.

The team worked to coax Maggie Lee's heart into a precocious stability. About an hour later, perhaps because I appeared too optimistic, the medical team—the doctor, nurses, a social worker, and a pediatric neurosurgeon who was on standby for the craniotomy that did not happen—called John and me into the family room for a conference.

The pediatric ICU doctor began by explaining the severity of Maggie Lee's injuries. They were very profound, and we should not expect her to make it through the night. In our shock, we tried desperately to absorb the information and John formulated questions.

The team was aware that John was a pastor and had seen the large crowd gathered in the waiting area with little groups of three to five people praying for Maggie Lee to survive. The doctors wanted to make clear that we should have little hope. Increasingly plainspoken, they emphasized that Maggie Lee's brain was profoundly damaged and that she would not live. When we asked a question that reflected any amount of hope for Maggie Lee's survival, the doctors exchanged looks and explained again. Finally, the irritated neurosurgeon said that there was no hope for survival and that, even if she did somehow make it, she would never be able even to blink to communicate with us.

John asked excellent questions, and I explained that I heard what they were saying but that we believed that God could do anything. I was not arguing with science, but in my book, there is *always* room for hope—a philosophy I still absolutely cling to. I took notes at the meeting because I wanted to be able to report the correct information to my family and friends. When the meeting was over, John and I looked at each other with extreme disbelief and brokenness.

We wept as the sun set on the worst day of our lives. How could this be real? The team told us that we needed to tell our family, so we went to the packed waiting area and told them that Maggie Lee was not expected to make it through the night. I prayed for strength to deliver the news.

That night as I was alone with my mother, I said, "If she dies tonight, she will die knowing just how much I love her." Although I am far from perfect, I have loved my kids with all of my heart every single day of their lives. While everything within me begged for a miracle, I knew if Maggie Lee's earthly days were over, then I had done that one job right.

Chapter 3

Week One

Despite all odds, Maggie Lee made it through the night. The doctor insisted on getting a CT scan to see how much damage had been done from the lack of oxygen to her brain and determine what we were dealing with. The challenge would be keeping her alive while moving her from the PICU in Batson Children's to the first-floor CT scan in the ER department, clear across the hospital.

The team of nurses and doctors discussed the game plan and then loaded her two poles full of tubes and took along portable paddles in case she crashed on the way down. They had to make sure that her collapsed lung stayed inflated. We all just prayed that Maggie Lee would make it. Our faithful friends and family stood silently as the stretcher rolled past with poles and the organized chaos of nurses and doctors as John and I silently followed.

We prayed as we walked, rode the elevator, and maneuvered the twists and turns down to the machine. The doctor cursed at the stray linen hamper obstructing our way. Maggie Lee arrived at the destination alive. The next challenge was lifting her from the gurney into the CT scan machine. There was no room for parents in the tiny space, so we stayed outside in the ER waiting area. I glanced up to notice the overhead TV tuned to a local news station whose lead line was "Church Bus Wreck." With Maggie Lee's picture as well as the horrible image of the mangled bus overhead (the first time I had seen the graphic picture), I prayed that I would see her precious smile again.

Loud but calm directions came one after another as the staff propped open the door and wheeled the gurney out of the CT scan room. John and I breathed a sigh of relief that our daughter was still alive. I remember having seen children in the halls of Batson's

Children's Hospital with a far-off look and just one usable hand to control a wheelchair and thought, "I'll take it, Lord. Just please let her live." We gladly would have cared for her in any form just to have her with us.

Snaking through the hospital once more, we rounded the corner in front of the waiting room to the obvious relief of our loved ones. They rejoiced that Maggie Lee had survived the CT scan. Since she was not even supposed to make it this far, who knew what else was possible?

Back at her spot in the PICU and during the rest of Monday, Maggie Lee miraculously seemed to stabilize. Nurse Lindsay suggested that John and I set up a CaringBridge.org site for Maggie Lee to disseminate information to a lot of people at once. That way, people could know exactly how to pray for Maggie Lee. I was familiar with CaringBridge; my friend Kenn's daughter had a site when she battled cancer.

That Tuesday with Maggie Lee's condition seemingly leveling off, John opened his laptop and in a few minutes set up a basic CaringBridge page for Maggie Lee. Within five minutes of listing the address on both of our Facebook pages, the CaringBridge site was flooded. People sent prayers, Bible verses, and encouraging messages to our daughter. Individuals from many different religions, Christian denominations, regions, and even countries were moved to pray for Maggie Lee.

We couldn't explain why so many people responded. We reasoned that with so many churches sending kids off to camp, the news must have hit home for parents all over the country. We read many CaringBridge messages recounting church services being interrupted to pray for our kids within minutes of the accident happening. The waiting room filled with people: family, friends, and even numerous strangers who came to offer support. Former Batson patients who had been given little hope for survival made the effort to come by and encourage us. For us, their very presence became hope incarnate.

My friend Andrea, whose brother is an ER physician, passed along this word of wisdom: "Some people come in with minor emergencies and die while other people you just know will die turn around and live. No one can say." And so while I listened carefully to the doctor's continued grim prognosis, I held on to that hope. Besides, I could not ask the mounting army of people praying for a miracle to believe in one if I did not believe in it myself.

During the first few days, Maggie Lee was given heavy sedation in an attempt to keep her brain as still as possible and control the intracranial pressure, or ICP. This medication induced her into a coma. Nearly midweek, the consensus was to peel back the medication to see if she still had brain activity. The concern with ICP is that with every spike, the brain is further injured.

We were told that ICP generally peaks within seventy-two hours, but for some reason Maggie Lee's would not come down. Her brain was too stubborn to reduce its swelling. Brain activity was evident, but her swelling was never under control. Maggie Lee's brain was angry, and her intracranial pressure continued creeping up.

One doctor was given the task of reviewing the CT scan with us. There in the nurses' station, he explained which part of her brain had sustained the bulk of the injury and how the damaged part had gotten worse since her initial scan in Meridian. He reassured me that because of her young age, the doctors were trying absolutely everything they could to give her a positive outcome. I was told that had she been an adult, they would not have fought this hard. Still, he showed little expectation that the effort would succeed. He kept saying things like "If she makes it," and "profoundly irreversible damage." The first week was as wretched as I could imagine; a week of utter devastation and hope beyond reason to hope.

Looking for hope, we forwarded hospital-issued copies of the CT scan pictures to two neurosurgeons for a second and third opinion. We sat with Maggie Lee and we waited. We prayed and wrote.

I just looked up at the clock and saw that it was 4:45 AM. It's maybe not so strange that I just happened to look up at the same time that I was getting Maggie Lee up to drive her to the church to board the bus for camp. We live less than five minutes from the church, so it wasn't going to be a problem to be there by the departure time.

I remember how excited Maggie Lee was to go to camp, but how sleepy she was at that hour. She got up, stepped into her clothes for the day, brushed her crazy hair, and then kissed what is most precious to her—Ellie the Chihuahua. If she could have fit the dog in her already overcrowded suitcase, she would have. And Ellie would have gladly obliged to be squeezed in just to be with her Maggie Lee.

I remember driving up and seeing that the parking lot was already full of kids. They looked like zombies standing there by the bus while their parents were dutifully filling out paperwork and wishing their kids were young enough to want to linger with them rather than grouping as they do with other youth and then lining up seating arrangements.

Maggie Lee had just gotten her braces put on a few days before and was supposed to take some pain reliever on the trip. When I realized that I had forgotten it, I boarded the bus before it left and told Maggie Lee that I didn't have it but that she could ask an adult for some if she started to hurt. Before leaving the bus, Jason (our youth minister at First Baptist Church of Shreveport) asked me if I would say a prayer for the trip.

I remember specifically praying for the safety of the bus, the driver, and the kids. I have gone back to that moment many times since the wreck, and the why of it all still lingers and dogs my mind and soul. I wonder if I said the right words, if I prayed specifically enough, if it mattered at all. The dogging, though, eventually gives way to a peace. While I do not understand how such a thing could happen, I am finding God's presence breaking through even in the roller-coaster agony of these days. (—John)

Chapter 4

Life in the PICU

Originally, we set up home base at the Cabot Lodge Hotel near the hospital. My mother, Judy Richardson; her twin sister, Aunt Jinny; my cousin Judy; Aunt Holly; John's father, Tom Henson; his father's wife, Sherolyn; and our son, Jack, filled several rooms. Northminster Baptist Church in Jackson adopted us, and after a week, several families offered their homes for us to stay in while they were on vacation. My brother Brink and my brother Ted's wife, Kelly, came to be with us that first week as well. Shawna and Stacie, friends whose sons were in school with Jack, and their families came from Shreveport to distract Jack, but he still spent many hours in the waiting area or back in the room with Maggie Lee. Home for us had always been wherever the four of us were, and now that foursome was seriously in question.

A church youth group was also staying at Cabot Lodge, and some of them, learning about what had happened, prayed for Maggie Lee right out in front of the waffle machine, God, and everybody. When you are desperate for a miracle, there is no such thing as pride.

My friends Gina R., Jen, Andrea, Colleen, Maureen, Kathy, and Gina C. set up a guest book underneath the pay phone (the only flat surface in the waiting nook) and distributed the CaringBridge site address they had copied on slips of paper to the many visitors. I always knew how blessed I was to have such strong, godly women at my side, but to have them drop their lives, find care for their children, and rearrange their work schedules to be with us in our most desperate hour was incredibly comforting. I deemed them my "Steel Magnolias," after the 1989 movie.

The hospital public relations team approached us. They had requests for television interviews for our family as well as those being treated in Jackson. Though thankful for prayer, we had no desire to be part of a press junket when our daughter was in such a devastating condition. We passed that duty to Gina Rees; John's father, Tom; and my mother, Judy, who did beautifully. The hospital was gracious in shielding us from further requests for interviews.

We continued to watch Maggie Lee's ICP, and our CaringBridge journals reflect the roller coaster of emotions we felt. Some entries in our guest book were from people whose children miraculously survived similar experiences, while others were from parents who ultimately had to turn off the machine because the pressure was never under control.

John and I continued our regimen of splitting the night shift, rotating around 1:00 a.m., with my mom and Aunt Jinny stepping in when we would allow it. My mom insisted on driving me and picking me up. Those who performed reinforcement duty after midnight would park at the basement entrance of Batson, which was locked at that time, and those completing the first shift would be waiting to open the locked automatic doors. Updates were given; the replacement would greet our sleeping Maggie Lee with fresh prayers and affection as the other tried to rest.

One of the most encouraging people in the hospital was a lady named Stacy. She was well over six feet tall and had a purposeful gait as she attended to the removal of trash cans overflowing with Kleenex and sanitized the area directly around the PICU patients. She had God's Spirit all over her and never passed John or me without offering a word of encouragement. "You don't give up on her, now," she would say. "Don't you get down, now." She nicknamed John "Superman" because of the red blanket he wrapped around himself late at night. I have always felt that the Lord uses us where we are and that everyone is called to ministry no matter where they work. This beautiful woman was evidence of that. I have often thought that she was far more of a chaplain to us than simply a member of the hospital housekeeping staff.

The pediatric ICU was cold and quiet at night except for the steady beat of the heart monitor and occasional alert that one of Maggie Lee's many medicines were nearing empty. She was given saline in an attempt to draw fluid off of her brain. With one sleepy eye on her ICP monitor, I would softly play Taylor Swift's *Fearless* CD, read Scripture, or read CaringBridge journal entries to Maggie Lee. Many times I would pray over her or have a one-sided conversation with her. I never dreamed how passionately I would long to see her indignant, preteen eye roll. Obviously, I would have given anything for her to wake up from the bad dream so we could all move forward with our happy lives.

Although Maggie Lee was fitted with leg-stimulator cuffs 24/7 to prevent blood clots, for brief times during the day, the nurses would let me take them off and massage her legs with lotion, which made me feel better. I would joke about her being stinky and assumed that she could hear and understand every word I said. For good measure, I painted her toenails and braided her hair in French braids. When I mentioned this on CaringBridge, many little girls responded with rally braids of their own as a show of support and a reminder to pray.

In addition to the leg-length cuffs, I could never get used to all the tubes connected to Maggie Lee. Since University Medical Center was a teaching hospital, med students would go on rounds with the doctors early in the morning. I began taking my bathroom breaks whenever they arrived at Maggie Lee's station because it was always awkward.

The doctor would lower his voice to a near whisper as the students leaned in and then stole a furtive glance my direction. I remember one incident in particular when a student exclaimed, "God, I've never seen anyone with two full poles before." The other students gave him the evil eye, and the teaching physician looked none too pleased.

We decorated Maggie Lee's station with some of the many handmade cards and pictures she received. Nurses Lindsay, Stacey, and Jessica helped me decorate one day, and their enthusiasm boosted my spirits immeasurably. I figured that if we were going to be there, I may as well make the space a little festive. I got peel-and-stick letters and put the phrase "Miracles Happen" on the dorm-sized window.

A steady stream of visitors from Shreveport on their way to vacation in Florida stopped by. Two of the youth from the bus, Lauren and Sara, were still in the hospital, as were an adult sponsor named Kyle, the youth minister, and several other youth. Some members of the youth group trickled in to visit, many of them traumatized. We were by no means the only ones devastated by this accident. What a living hell all of those on the bus must have endured.

The following is from my personal journal from that time. The many hours at Maggie Lee's bedside allowed me time to attempt to process my feelings through writing.

So many people have arrived to pray for us as well as for the miracle which we all know it would take for Maggie Lee to even live at this point. The gravity of her injuries has not escaped me, but still, if I lose hope for her, what else is left?

As the doctors examine her pupils and grunt, I know it is grave, but the person behind those eyes came from my body and is part of my soul.

They do not realize the hazel eyes which used to be baby blue when she was first born played "peep-eye" for her first trick or stared cock-eyed at herself in the mirror when she was three while modeling one of my bras. No, they look for lack of pupil reaction to light, which gives them the evidence that she is not in there. But they don't see. They can't.

I don't blame them; they cannot know how amazing she is. They cannot know how we have poured every ounce of the best we have to give into her. She is our Rembrandt, and so if appraisers come by and only see the damage, don't blame us if we disagree.

I certainly realize that the outcome is by no means up to me. I have fully accepted that. I trust God because He is good . . . all the time. (—Jinny)

CaringBridge

July 21, 2009

I was recently digging around in the outer flap of my computer bag. Some say it is my man bag, but I carry no such item. I was hunting for a cord for my computer; I found something I had not seen since early in this nightmare. It is a small Ziploc bag labeled "Specimen bag, Biohazard" that includes directions with four steps on how to insert something into it. Inside the bag is something very non-biohazardous, but something that must have been inserted with a few tears, a measure of compassion, and perhaps a prayer.

Inside the bag is a ring that Maggie Lee was wearing when they found her. It's a ring that Jinny bought for her when she was coming back recently from a trip to Knoxville, one to serve as an encircling reminder of how much she believes in Maggie Lee.

It was given to Maggie Lee to wear while going off to Camp Crestridge for two weeks of camp, where she didn't know anybody and would be 900 miles from home. Jinny knew she wouldn't know anyone at camp and wanted her to remember how much she believed in her and her dreams even though they would be apart.

Jinny is the greatest encourager I know. It's a gift of hers, and she is more than willing to pour it out liberally on anyone she sees. If you know Jinny, you will know that she is generous, loud, and completely heartfelt. It is fuel in my tank, and it is dispensed constantly in our house to accomplish anything from acing a math test to preaching a sermon or even to pulling a tooth.

I had no idea that she gave this ring to Maggie Lee, but it doesn't surprise me at all to learn of it tonight.

As I read the engraving, the words stood out to me, especially as I think of how they are so fitting of the way Maggie Lee lives her life. Engraved are these words: "Dream. Fly. Dance. Sing."

I am looking at my daughter now, asleep in the bed, knowing that it's not her time to go. Young, too full of dreams, flight, dance, and song. As I look at her beautiful, unusually quiet self resting in this bed, my prayer, O Lord, is for her to

Dream.

Fly.

Dance.

Sing.

May it be so, Lord God. May it be so.

"You turned my wailing into dancing; you removed my sack cloth and clothed me with joy," Psalm 30:11. (—John)

There were moments of lightness in this bleak time for us. While staying in the home of a Northminster Baptist member, our friends Gary and Sharon had come to visit to bring consolation and a cooler of Happy Bellies frozen custard, Maggie Lee's favorite Shreveport treat. Gary and John took the first vigil, and I took the second; Aunt Jinny picked me up when the nurses changed shifts and visitors were not allowed. John convinced Gary to stay at the house instead of making the four-hour drive back to Shreveport as was his original plan. It was still dark outside when I went to the master bedroom where John and I took turns sleeping. Jack was down the hall.

I entered the bedroom quietly so I would not disturb John, brushed my teeth, and faced the dresser to fold the blanket I had used for a shawl. John leaned up from the bed and asked how I was doing with his voice a bit lower than normal. I turned his direction and, noticing that something was off, I asked, "Did you get a haircut yesterday?" Then realization dawned on me. Horrified that I was mere feet away from a bed where another woman's husband had been sleeping, I bolted from the room screaming, "Gary Mazzanti's in my bed!" and ran down the hall.

The whole house woke up to my shrieks. Everyone was relieved to learn it was a mere misunderstanding. It gave way to roaring laughter—a glorious exercise we needed desperately.

Chapter 5

Jairus and a Chihuahua

The third week at Batson Children's Hospital in Jackson was almost more intense than the beginning of our ordeal. The doctors explained to us that Maggie Lee was not responding to the treatment at all, that it was time to stop "chasing the ICP and let her declare herself one way or another." They finally allowed us to have one of the few rooms in the PICU with actual walls, allowing for a blessed shred of the privacy we so desired.

Doctors explained that a change in strategy was warranted. Even with the massive amounts of drugs used to sedate her and the saline given to draw fluids from her brain, Maggie Lee's intracranial pressure was still astronomical, creeping into the 40s and beyond when the average is 12. This caused continued insult to her already injured brain.

They theorized that she was having a continuous stream of strokes, and that was why her brain was so swollen. We had consulted with neurosurgeons Dr. Anil Nanda of Shreveport and Dr. David Cavanaugh, and they both agreed that everything that could possibly be done was done. The only thing left to do was pray. There was no plan B.

I still remember and am informed by Dr. Nanda's words to me in one conversation. "You have to consider that even if she were to survive, would you want her to be unable to respond to you, unable to play with her friends?" he asked. "Would you want that kind of existence for yourself?" I hung on his every word, and since he was the head of neurosurgery at Louisiana State University, I knew he had dealt skillfully with thousands of brain-injury cases. He was kind, empathetic, and a man of deep belief in God.

Meanwhile, thousands more joined the prayer efforts for Maggie Lee. Signs reading, "Pray for Maggie Lee . . . Miracles Happen," surfaced in yards across the Shreveport-Bossier area as well as in the Dallas-Ft. Worth Metroplex. I still believed that God could perform a miracle for Maggie Lee if He chose. I also believed that this would be an excellent time for God to show off with something only He could do. Once more, God was veering from the great marketing plan I thought God should follow if he wanted people to be impressed.

I had never wanted something more in my life than for Maggie Lee to live. Forget all of the hopes and dreams of honor roll, Broadway, or a wedding. At this point, my dream was just for our daughter to breathe on her own. I would more than gladly give my life in exchange for hers, but that is not the way things work. Of course, that doesn't mean you don't think about them and pray for them, as anyone who has been blindsided by life will tell you.

If the accident taught me anything, it was about the complete lack of control I have over any aspect of my life. I thought that by playing by the rules and teaching my children to avoid strangers or by accompanying them to the public rest room when their friends were long since allowed to go by themselves would keep them safe. I realized that despite how much we insulate ourselves, control is truly just a façade. Even though I had done all I could to ensure Maggie Lee's long and healthy life on earth, I realized that, in a matter of a few days, her soul could be in heaven.

Our friend Donna Cavanaugh sent us the book *Go Back and Be Happy: Reclaiming Life after a Devastating Loss* by Julie Papievis (Oxford: Monarch Books, 2008). The book details Julie's experience of dying and going to heaven and then returning to earth. Her brain injuries were obviously less severe than Maggie Lee's, but she wrote about the anguish of returning to earth and the brutal rehabilitation that awaited her—along with depression over returning to earth when heaven was so blissful.

Not so blissful were our meetings with the doctors that third week. Every encounter revolved around decisions we might have to make should they peel back the sedation and find that Maggie Lee still had brain activity. Since she was tube fed and on a ventilator, she was artificially kept alive. We would have to decide to continue or discontinue these measures depending on what the tests revealed. I never gave up hope that our miracle could happen, but as the week progressed, a miracle seemed less and less likely.

CaringBridge

Monday, July 27, 2009 6:05 AM, CDT

I can't get Jairus out of my head these days. That crazy name has been bouncing around in there each of these last 15 days.

It wasn't too many weeks ago in the lectionary that I preached from the passage in Mark (5:22-43) that gives us just a small yet magnificent glimpse into Jairus's life.

My focus was on the story within the story, about the woman who had a bleeding disorder and who reached out to touch the hem of Jesus' garment. All of this happened between the time that Jesus received Jairus's plea for him to heal his daughter to the time that Jesus actually arrived at the bedside of Jairus's daughter to perform the healing.

In light of what has happened in my life since preaching this text, perhaps I should have focused on the Jairus end of the story. Who knew I would have so much in common with a man named Jairus?

So, out of the inability to get Jairus out of my head, I return to Mark 5. What strikes me most is something that hit me while studying the text several weeks ago—Jairus's daughter was 12 years old. I think I even remember noting in my sermon, even though it's not in my manuscript, of how it struck me that our daughters were the same age. I've read and studied this passage countless times, but this time, in this twelfth year of my daughter, it grabbed me in a new way, and I could relate to him and imagine what he was going through. And now, that identification is even greater. I now read this passage with a kind of association I would rather not have.

I am right there with Jairus now at the feet of Jesus, pleading earnestly with this Jesus whom I've seen and whom I've known to do great miracles. I am right there in my desperation and utter fear, realizing that there is nothing else that can work and no one else who can help. I'm right there, not worried about what others who consider it futile or even foolish to go to Jesus are thinking. I'm at the feet of Jesus, and I'm pleading. I'm right there believing that there is power in the hands of Jesus and that their placement on my daughter will mean that "she will be healed and live."

I also identify with what must have been great impatience on the part of Jairus when he saw Jesus taking time to stop and relate to someone else. I'm sure he was thinking, "Uh . . . um, excuse me, Jesus, what are you doing? My daughter is dying and you don't have time for anything else." Jesus didn't seem to be bothered by the urgency of the situation but was, rather, confident that he (and she) was right in God's timing. Healing was on the way but had not fully arrived.

I, even at this very moment, feel tremendous urgency and the stress of timing. I fear the unknown while my daughter sleeps and find myself pulling on the other side of Jesus' garment to get him moving; I want him to do something visible right now. Right now, Jesus! Jesus, don't you know about ICPs and CPPs? Don't you know what will happen if those numbers keep spiraling upward?

Jairus and my soul are reminding me to be patient, that healing is on its way.

Meanwhile, I'm inserting myself into this passage and will keep this Jairus prayer going until I see the results of "Talitha koum!" manifest in my daughter's body.

Jesus, "my little daughter is dying. Please come and put your hands on her so that she will be healed and live." (—John)

Well into our third week, intensely sleep deprived and hopped up on hospital coffee, I made a unilateral decision: it was time for Ellie the Chihuahua to see Maggie Lee. Since she was finally in a room of her own, I figured a reunion was in order. John thought this was a bad idea and would have no part of it. Then again, due to his common sense, he originally was against the idea of a third dog in our house. In fall 2008, Maggie Lee begged for months for a Chihuahua. Since she rarely asked for anything, I was all for the idea.

When John finally relented, he called her into his room and said, "Maggie Lee, you have been asking for a dog for months."

"Yes sir, I know. I will stop." She sighed in obedient resignation.

"I've thought about this, and we are going to let you get a Chihuahua, but since we already have two other dogs, I'm considering this a cat."

She was so giddy that we raced out that very day to secure a six-week-old puppy for her. Maggie Lee named her Elle Woods after Reese Witherspoon's character in *Legally Blonde*, one of our favorite movies. Ellie became Maggie Lee's constant companion as well as a source of unconditional love and friendship.

By the time Maggie Lee was in her own room in the pediatric ICU, Ellie had been separated from her for nearly three weeks. My second cousin, Poem, who lived outside of Jackson, graciously kept Ellie, but I wanted Ellie at least to know where Maggie Lee had been.

Sneaking Ellie into Maggie Lee's room involved a backpack, a loquacious grandmother, and some quick negotiations by a ten-year-old brother. "I just don't think this is a good idea, Jinny," my mother, "Mimi," kept repeating, clutching her stomach as we stuffed the dog in Jack's backpack and headed for the first-floor elevators. From her anxiety level, one would have thought we were trying to pull off a jewel heist at the Tower of London.

Fully ignoring her misgivings, I repeated the game plan: "Mother, stall the nurses . . . ask lots of questions and act natural. It is *fine*. What are they going to do to us at this point, kick us out?" We approached the hall where the nurses sat monitoring vitals via remote just outside Maggie Lee's room. Instead of the customary two, there was only one nurse.

Panic.

Jack and I entered Maggie Lee's room while Mimi tried her best to act natural and nervously talked Nurse Lindsay's ear off. Our other nurse was inside the room checking all kinds of monitors and rear-ranging the sheets. She would not leave.

Jack skillfully cradled the backpack, scooted the heavy chair-bed away from the nurses' sight, and muffled Ellie's squeals as much as possible. All in all, we were absolutely miserable liars. Nurse Stacey finally left, and when the coast was clear, Jack extracted Ellie from the backpack and stuck her in the hospital bed. I then obscured the nurses' view with my body.

I wasn't sure if the nurses turned a blind eye or if we had actually successfully sneaked a dog into the pediatric ICU of Batson Children's Hospital. Either way, Ellie snuggled under the sheets and came to rest on the warm yet still body of the girl she loved so dearly. We allowed Ellie to remain twenty minutes, which was about as long as my mother could stand being a rule-breaker.

Aside from the blessing of finally having a private room, the week droned on and on. Because she was on pain medication, I did not worry about Maggie Lee feeling pain. Instead, I worried about her not feeling anything at all. The medical staff "peeled back the sedation" for a full five days due to the heavy dosage of drugs the needed to wear off to provide an accurate assessment.

On Sunday, August 2, Dr. Christ performed the standard bedside test for brain death, and with no reflexes or pupil movement detected, she determined that our daughter was no longer with us. For our benefit, the doctor ordered a radioactive dye test to measure blood flow to the brain. The results would be called up to the pediatric ICU immediately following the test, and if she was indeed brain dead, the time of death would be the time the phone call was made.

The results came back at 6:30 p.m., August 2, 2009—our first-born child's time of death.

We had a myriad of decisions before us. The most pressing one was whether or not we should donate Maggie Lee's organs.

Not considering myself a selfish person, in my heart I thought, "Hasn't her little body been through enough?" I was beyond ready to leave Mississippi and just go home. Then, as John and I scribbled our lists of pros and cons—just as we had during our fifteen years of marriage for far more trivial decisions—John in all of his wisdom brought up an undeniable point.

"You know, Maggie Lee would give anything she had to someone who needed it."

In my sleep-deprived mind flashed numerous scenarios of her generosity—giving Christmas money so that our World Vision child in remote India could have school supplies; picking out a stuffed animal monkey when she learned that sweet Mary, the school custodian, collected them; offering her allowance when Jack saw something at Target he wanted. She was not a perfect child, but she had a spontaneous, God-given generosity, and I knew that we needed to honor it.

My first real job was in the public relations department of Baylor University Medical Center the week before Mickey Mantle received his controversial liver transplant. I had even helped launch his family's organ-donation drive through "Mickey's Team," but now that I had a chance to offer our child's battered body, it was suddenly a profoundly difficult decision. Still, overall, I could not deny that Maggie Lee would want to save someone's life if she could. We decided that organ donation was what she would want.

We answered the battery of questions, obviously intended for an older organ donor. "No, she never had hepatitis." "No, she did not drink alcohol." "No, she did not exchange sex for drugs in the past six weeks." I winced at that one. Her premature death would mean that I would never get to hear my daughter's story about her first kiss.

We took care of those details, and John decided he would stay with Maggie Lee until the doctors flew in for surgery. Jack, Aunt Jinny, my mom, my sister-in-law Theresa, and I returned to our borrowed home base.

While John waited vigilantly with our daughter, he updated CaringBridge with our bad news. Of course, word had already spread that she was gone.

CaringBridge

August 2, 2009

At 6:30 tonight, our precious Maggie Lee was carried into the arms of her Lord and Savior Jesus Christ. For these last three weeks, she fought for her life courageously, with the skillful help of the medical staff at Batson Children's Hospital here in Jackson. She was blessed to have thousands of people praying and pulling for her. We celebrate her eternal life in the presence of her Creator tonight.

We gathered around Maggie Lee with this beautiful prayer from the Book of Common Prayer:

Into your hands, O merciful Savior, we commend your servant Maggie Lee. Acknowledge, we humbly beseech you, a sheep of your own fold, a lamb of your own flock, a sinner of your own redeeming. Receive her into the arms of your mercy, into the blessed rest of everlasting peace, and into the glorious company of the saints in light. Amen.

May her soul and the souls of all the departed, through the mercy of God, rest in peace. Amen.

We will be posting plans for her Celebration of Life in Shreveport, Louisiana, as details are completed. Thank you for your constant love and support.

In keeping with the giving spirit of Maggie Lee, we are currently in the process of determining organ donation. For that reason, we will not be going back to Shreveport until Monday evening or Tuesday. (—John)

John stayed with Maggie Lee's body through the night as the surgeons flew in from three different states to harvest what would be other peoples' miracles. We prayed that those who would get Maggie Lee's organs would have successful transplants and the new shot at life they so desired.

Chapter 6

Doodle Bugs in a Shoe Box

We loaded up in the Odyssey minivan we had bought two months earlier to have room for our two children and their friends. I felt swallowed up in a vehicle we no longer needed. We sleepily gathered our belongings and, in a daze, we packed up to leave Jackson, Mississippi. Despite the hospitable new friends and skillful medical staff, it will forever be to me the place where my daughter died.

With my dutiful mother and her sister distributing leftover snacks to the homeless shelter and taking care of thank-you notes, we drove. With the knowledge that organ recovery surgery was complete, we left for home as Maggie Lee's body was released for transportation to the funeral home in Shreveport.

Only a month before, we had driven the same stretch of interstate to bring the kids back from summer camp in Asheville, North Carolina. After camp, Maggie Lee had spent a week in Dallas at an intense acting workshop with her friend, Reagan. Now, instead of decisions about voice lessons and acting classes, we had to decide on caskets, burial plots, and who would preach at her graveside service. How could this be?

Once home on Monday, we were greeted by a clean house, meals, and cards. Even in our shock, we were grateful for these things. The three of us ambled around our two-story house like doodle bugs in a shoe box. The saying, "You can ignore someone's presence, but it is impossible to ignore someone's absence," rang true as we wandered in the deafening silence.

On Tuesday, we met the funeral director and, since the bus wreck was such a publicized story, the owner of the funeral home. We made decisions regarding what type of casket, what color liner, and how to fix her hair. The older gentleman suggested that perhaps, since Maggie Lee had so much hair in the back, the beautician could somehow swing some across the front to cover the shaved spot and stitches. I was thinking, "If you try to give my daughter a comb-over, mister, she *will* rise up out of that casket and get you." Luckily for John, I didn't say it.

John's fortieth birthday was August 5. I had planned a surprise party for him, but I had not told the kids because keeping secrets was never Maggie Lee's forte. I could envision her ratting me out, and I didn't want to risk it. With the delay due to organ transportation and the fact that no one wanted the service to be on John's birthday, we decided on August 6 for Maggie Lee's Celebration of Life Service. Unfortunately, there was a visitation to fit in, and so that was held on August 5.

The entire evening was surreal: from seeing her name on the interchangeable black marquee just outside the visitation room, to the throngs of florists' cards with our names on them, to the reactions on our family's and her friends' faces. I tried to comfort her cousins by likening her body to the shell of a hermit crab when he had no use for it any longer. We greeted the hundreds of people who waited for hours in the brutal summer heat and were surrounded by our families and my "Steel Magnolias"—the seven women who dropped their lives to support us in Jackson.

Surrounded by my friends at the visitation, I watched as Kathy Carlisle shoved Gina Rees in front of me and said, "Hit her!" reminiscent of the graveside scene in the film *Steel Magnolias*. We laughed a huge, refreshing laugh for which we were starved. Laughter is one of God's greatest gifts, and I had never needed it more than that night.

We returned home, and I urged John to open his birthday presents from his father even though none of us had ever felt more miserable. He halfheartedly unwrapped his gifts and we tried to get ready for bed. As I lay down, the gut-wrenching, animalistic weeping poured forth from my spirit as I faced the truth that my beloved daughter was dead.

The Celebration of Life service on August 6 truly was that. We asked a few of Maggie Lee's friends to speak, and her brother Jack bravely offered to say something as well. He read one of thousands of tributes to Maggie Lee posted on CaringBridge:

> Dear Maggie Lee,
>
> I wanted to thank you for inspiring so many people to have hope and faith. Christian and I have been glued to the computer since we heard the sad news. I have to confess that I was not as lucky as you to be brought up in church. I have always thought of myself as a Christian, but never really gone to church or been routine about praying. I confess this to you to explain what an impact you have made on Christian and myself. While we were at the prayer service at Trophy Club last night in your honor, we both felt God's presence. What an amazing feeling! We felt all of the love and support in the room. God was there with us and he was listening to our prayers. God is working through *you*! We thank you for your strength and bravery. We will continue to pray for the swelling to decline. Thank you for your guidance.
>
> We love you,
> Marcie and Christian Conrad (posted to CaringBridge on Thursday, July 16, 2009)

Jack then ended with these words: "Anyone who got to know Maggie knew that she wanted to be a singer and actress when she grew up. But instead, God used her to show thousands of people his love and mercy." His composure was especially inspiring considering that the last time he had been in the sanctuary, he had heard the announcement that the bus had flipped.

Several of Maggie Lee's friends, Camille Carlisle, Reagan Rees, and Elizabeth Burgess, as well as her "twin cousin," Madeline, spoke. These are her poignant words:

> My dearest, sweetest cousin, Maggie Lee,
>
> Wow. What a roller coaster ride these past few weeks have been. I'm still trying to slow down and take it all in. I just can't come to believe I'm up here giving a memorial speech at your Celebration of Life. I often stopped and wondered, "Why? Why Maggie Lee? What

did she ever do wrong?" I may not understand until I'm up with you and God in heaven. All I know for now is it's all just part of God's plan.

Just think, a month ago, we sat together at the Fourth of July fireworks. We joked around, laughed, and even did a little dance together. I'm forcing myself to believe all of this, but as hard as I try, it's just not possible.

Maggie Lee, your life here on earth was way too short, but it was jam-packed full of memories that will last a lifetime. One of my earliest memories is of you and me sitting on your porch in Floresville blowing bubbles together. We were probably just under two years old. Then, a few years later, we looked so much alike that we decided that we just had to be twins. The only problem was, twins were sisters, not cousins. No problem! Let's call ourselves "twin cousins"!

I remember birthday parties and holidays and everything in between. I'll remember cooking in Mimi's kitchen. Never having the right ingredients, we would always substitute or go next door and get what we needed. I never quite understood how a chocolate-chip cookie recipe could lead us to make what was more like a chocolate-chip soup!

Maggie Lee, your fun, bubbly personality made you someone who will never be forgotten. I remember you telling me that you wanted to be famous, to be a star one day. A real star is someone who touches people's hearts and has accomplished great things. You did exactly those things. You've touched the hearts of people you've never even met.

You've also accomplished more in a few weeks than most people accomplish in a lifetime. You have brought families closer together and also closer to God. On top of that, you've also saved two lives! You may not have received the miracle you wanted, but you provided miracles for two other children through organ donation. Maggie Lee, you truly are a star.

I often wonder, "Why does it all have to end like this?" Lack of prayer? No, hundreds of thousands of people out there are praying for you. Lack of faith? No, not that either. These past few weeks, myself, along with many others have been brought closer to God than we have ever been. I've learned to completely put my faith and trust in God.

Then again, I realized, it's just all a part of God's plan. A plan I truly don't understand now. But I do know that God does everything for a reason. I know you are up there in heaven with Jesus now, at a welcome party thrown just for you. Pop and Golly must be happy to have their granddaughter up there with them.

Maggie Lee, although your soul left this earth, I know a part of you will always remain with me. You're my twin cousin, you're my best friend. I love you, Maggie Lee, and I'll miss you forever,

Madeline

From Reagan Rees:

Maggie—my mentor!
Here are the things I have learned from you so far:

- Laugh a lot
- Take risks without being embarrassed
- Don't let mean people get you down
- Be happy being you (me)
- Love Chihuahuas
- Stop dog nudity—dress your dog in the best fashions!
- You're never fully dressed without a smile

I love you! I love you!

Your Bestest friend/fan,
Reagan :)

Elizabeth, Maggie's dear friend from school, read beautifully from Proverbs 3:5-6. She was Maggie Lee's best friend here and as faithful, sweet, and good as a friend could ever be.

Lisa Alford, Maggie Lee's choir teacher and beloved friend, read 2 Timothy 4:7.

Leah, Maggie Lee's voice coach, sang "For Good."

Pastor Greg did a sweet job of summing up Maggie Lee's life as the shadow of a flashing comet, describing her sparkling nature and the impact she had on those around her.

Jason, the youth minister, said prayers for the family in his gracious way, and Randy, the music minister, led a stirring rendition of "It Is Well with My Soul." This song was written by Horatio Spafford in 1873 when he was grieving the deaths of his daughters Annie, Bessie, Tanetta, and Margaret Lee (remarkably, our Maggie Lee's given name).

All three of Maggie Lee's uncles: John's older brother, Scott Henson; and my brothers Brink and Ted Richardson; along with Don Blair, Al Cook, J. J. Jangula, Mike Woods, and Gary Mazzanti were pallbearers.

Enclosed in the program was a poem I had written for Maggie Lee in 2006 titled "You Are My Prize."

I want to clear up something
I think you have misheard,
When I tuck you in at night
And fill you with my words.
I say I am so proud to have
A child so bright and sweet.
With excellent report cards
Which knock me off my feet!
Oh, how your fresh eyes sparkle,
Your grin lights up a room.
Your spirit beams as brightly,
As a Carolina moon.
Your tenderness to others
Is truly rare these days.
I love to see your kindness
And your sweet, caring ways.
Your taste in clothes is stellar,
Your acting skills immense,
But what if, come tomorrow,
You lost that fashion sense?
If your lovely hair fell out,

Those sparkling eyes turned bland,
If you saw a mean kid throw a punch,
And did not take a stand.
If instead of A's and B's,
Your report card was a mess,
If you, no longer at the top,
Were called the worst, not best.
If all these bad things happened,
(This part might shock you here)
To me you'd be as beautiful,
Absolutely as dear.
It's fun to try your hardest,
Good work has its rewards.
But that's not why you're special
To me or to The Lord.
You'll see when you get older,
And then for sure you'll know,
It is not what your children DO
That makes you love them so.
You are not what you do, my love,
Life is so much more
Than any outward beauty
Or excellent test score.
I know you love to come in first,
You have right from the start.
But never, ever be confused,
You already have my heart.
I love you, precious person,
Just the way you are.
You need not paint me pictures
Or play me your guitar.
So try new things with gusto!
Fail and fail again.
It's only those who never try
Who miss out on the win.
Don't judge yourself too harshly,
Enjoy the journey, too.
Laugh along the way each day,

I hear it's good for you.
You could not be more wonderful,
More precious in my eyes.
If you never won again,
You still would be my prize.

After the Celebration of Life service, I returned to a house full of people with my family bustling around, replacing the honey baked ham and napkin supply. I took several of my friends who had never been to my Shreveport home to see Maggie Lee's room. Just the Christmas before, I had redecorated it with a Broadway theme, complete with a wall of mirrors, rope lights, and stage curtains. I found ten-inch letters at the craft store with which I spelled "BROADWAY." She adored her yellow room and spent many hours singing, dancing, and acting in her bedroom.

I kept thinking that Maggie Lee would have loved a party like this, with all of her favorite people assembled in one place. We saw church members from every church we'd served, and I wondered who had thought to invite them. There were so many more I should have asked to come. The unreality of the day continued as the house emptied and the actual graveside service loomed. One more day and I could crash, I thought.

On August 7, 2009, we held the graveside service in Tyler, Texas, for Maggie Lee. John's mother is buried in Roseview Cemetery there, and so we found four plots together and purchased them for our family. Bill Heston, a Presbyterian minister friend of ours, performed the meaningful service. The heat was oppressive, and the Astroturf beneath my black pumps didn't prevent them from digging into the fertile East Texas soil.

We laid flowers on the casket, prayed again to a God who had never heard so many constant petitions from us, and made our way to First Baptist Church of Tyler (John's home church) for lunch. Nancy Crawford and other friends of John's parents had prepared a wonderful meal for us, and we ate what we could.

Relieved that at least now the public events were over, we headed east on I-20 for the ninety minutes it took to get to Shreveport. Now began the daunting task of living a life I had no desire to live, being the kind of parent that my son deserved, and attempting to glorify a God whose actions I did not understand. I knew I lacked the strength to do any of it.

In the first few weeks, I had to occupy myself. Thank-you notes were an excellent place to start. My mother was a huge help, and even though her heart was breaking, she served all of us with her typical iron-clad strength. I sent the jeweler, Amy Peters, John's story about finding Maggie Lee's ring because I wanted her to know what an inspiration her work had been to us.

The family of Brandon, the only other youth who died as a result of the wreck, chose to move away the first week of school. Understandably, they wanted to leave Shreveport and the horror here in their rearview mirror. Since we had never met them, John and I wanted to visit with his parents, John and Jenny, before they left the state. Our visit was brief, as their house was mainly boxed up already. We listened to their stories about their oldest child—his grades and ambitions. We found ourselves, like so many of our friends in this situation, without the right words to say.

In some instances, there are no words.

Chapter 7

Questions for God: An Interlude

As my voice enters into the book with this chapter, the different responses Jinny and I have had to Maggie Lee's death will no doubt be obvious. They are similar in many ways, yet as different as the two of us are from one another. It doesn't take long for anyone to see that we are polar opposites, which is a strength of our marriage. The questions I have for God in this chapter are ones we have both asked, though we have presented them to God in our very different ways. We have both found help accepting them, even as we have each drawn support and encouragement in our own ways. Sharing these questions and our sources of help has only provided strength and support to our marriage.

While a long list of questions has come up since July 12, 2009, the two biggest ones are for God: "Why did you allow this?" and "Where were you?"

Question 1: Why Did God Allow This?

It's an age-old question, typically asked with an eye to the sky, a clinched fist held upward, a heart beating with emotion, and a gut twisting with the feeling of betrayal and possibly even disbelief. It is a question people no doubt continue to ask day after day as circumstances beyond our control happen to us or to others around us.

I guess I am still asking this question, although I think I have come to the realization that I won't have an answer this side of heaven. It comes to me often on Sunday afternoons, in the time away from work, the time we would spend together as a family, jumping on the trampoline or just collapsing in front of the random selection of TV shows typical of a Sunday afternoon. The question of why sometimes comes to me as I walk into Maggie Lee's room, thinking of the life that was once there and noticing the quiet filling it now. Or it sneaks up on me at times when I see one of her friends, wondering if Maggie Lee would be involved in the same things they are now; wondering if she would be as tall as some; wondering which high school she would have attended. I also ask "Why?" in the mornings, usually in that moment between waking up and actually getting out of bed, when thoughts come without any context or reason, indicating that such a question needs not be pricked by a memory only but is being asked subconsciously even while I sleep.

The question comes up at other times as I work with people who are also asking the question, or as my friends ask it in their own lives. In 2011, I lost a close friend—Jay Greenleaf—who was also a church member. I suddenly found myself relating to the question both as a care giver and as an individual in grief. The circumstances of his death truly led to such a question, as he was a young, caring, generous person who was in the prime of his life, making an ongoing impact in our city, in our church, in his family, and in so many other ways. His life abruptly and strangely ended as he was out playing golf after work, electrocuted by a lightning bolt that appeared out of nowhere. This was another event in life that made no sense. We were all wondering why God would allow this to happen. I began my sermon at Jay's funeral service, looking out at a packed sanctuary of people still stunned by what had happened to this man so full of life.

"What happened?" That's a question on all our hearts, minds, and tongues as we try to make sense of it all. There is a deeper question. "Why, God, did you allow this to happen?" We won't know that answer this side of heaven. What we can know, though, is found in John 11:17-37, which tells the story of the death and resurrection of Jesus' friend, Lazarus. Lazarus, a friend of Jesus, had become sick and died. His sisters, Mary and Martha, also friends of Jesus, were bewildered with the shock and irrationality of death. The sisters called on Jesus to heal their brother, but Jesus didn't get there in time. The sisters' anger and bitterness at the perceived lack of urgency is apparent in Martha's statement, "Lord, if you had been here, my brother would not have died" (John 11:21 NRSV). This is the same type of statement I think all of us gathered in the sanctuary at Jay Greenleaf's funeral wanted to say to God. Why, God? Why didn't you get here earlier? It was a feeling much like we had when we first learned of the bus accident, but particularly during the three weeks we continued to call on God to show up and heal Maggie Lee.

Common Responses

It Was God's Will

Nearly everyone who has grieved knows that there is always at least one person in the visitation line who takes the angle that the death was God's will. This is usually said with compassion and encouragement, yet the words leave the bereaved feeling empty and bitter at a God who would will such a thing. The verse this person often cites is Romans 8:28, "We know that all things work together for good for those who love God, who are called according to his purpose (NRSV). The person interprets this verse as saying that God caused a death because it was God's will rather than saying God's hand is not in the cause but in the good that can come out of all things. In our first days and even year of grief, it was not uncommon to hear this response about God's will. Even with seminary training and eighteen years of ministry experience, knowing I will hear this and being certain that it is not true, the words still confuse and hurt me.

I remember wondering about this frequent statement while I was sitting at Maggie Lee's bedside one night. She was deep in a coma, the floor was quiet, and it was early in the morning. As the thought ran across my mind, I couldn't bring myself to any understanding or interest in a God who would do such a thing to my child simply because it was his will. People in Old Testament times viewed God this way, but Jesus' revelation of God is the clearest picture of God. In my view, a capricious God who blows out tires, flips buses, and causes traumatic brain injuries doesn't gel with how Jesus represents God.

God Allowed It to Happen to Reach People

Another common response is also said with the goal of comfort. It is usually phrased this way: "But just think of all those who wouldn't have heard about Jesus if this hadn't happened" or "I think God wanted this to happen to bring people to Jesus." While I do believe—as one can see throughout this book—that God can and will bring good out of any bad thing that happens, this kind of response also fails to comfort those in grief. Yes, I want people to come to Jesus, but doesn't God have some other way than causing a horrific accident and the deaths of children? Does God really desire for someone to develop cancer cells and suffer through years of surgery and chemotherapy just to bring people to Jesus?

God Allowed or Caused It to Happen to Receive Glory

The next response is more about God being glorified than people coming to faith in Jesus. The idea here is that God causes tragedies or even positive events in order to bring glory to God's name. It's as if God has this huge ego and a self-centered need to get all the attention of everyone on earth. It fails to allow for the clearest picture of God we have, one where God enters earth not rich or self-seeking, but poor and selfless throughout his life. God entered our world by taking the form of a servant and, ultimately, dying on a cross. If there were ever an event for God to get glory, it was through the life, death, and resurrection of Jesus. Does God still need to allow or cause suffering, tragedy, or even good things to give him glory?

God Wants to Get Our Attention

Some people respond to tragedy by saying, "God caused or allowed this death to happen to teach a lesson or to get our attention." While this is said with no obvious intention of providing comfort, it is said nonetheless. I can't remember anyone saying these exact words to us directly, but I think that was the message we were to hear through a few indirect responses. It tends to come from super-spiritual types of people, those who seem to know exactly what God is doing at any given time and have no problem telling people what God is trying to say. To the bereaved, this response implies that God cares more for the person who needs the lesson than for the life God snuffs out to teach the lesson. Again, in this response God is capricious and willing to use whatever means to justify the end. This view is at the heart of the book of Job, giving God the role of making a deal with the devil in order to prove that there is someone who will love and praise God, even if that person loses everything. Job indeed loses his children, his wealth, his health, and his reputation. God wins in the end, but only at the end of a trail strewn with boils, suffering, and death.

God Is Mad

Another common response is not usually heard (unless you have friends like Job's), but it is often thought in relation to the deceased. "I guess that person must have done something wrong," some people say. "God must be punishing him/her." This cause-and-effect thinking flows out of our primitive religious roots. If your town is conquered, then your town deserved it. If you get sick and die, you must have done something to anger the gods. If your crops die, the god of wheat is angry and needs a sacrifice in order to be happy with you again. It is our attempt to explain the inexplicable in life. Death didn't make sense to our ancestors long ago, and it still doesn't make sense today. We need a reason. Understanding it as a result of our actions is our instinctive, convenient response, and so we go with it. And this is as far as some people get.

God Is Not Real or Just Doesn't Care

Although I haven't heard this said aloud about our tragedy, it is a conclusion many people make in such circumstances: "God is either not real or doesn't care; otherwise, he would have intervened and prevented it." This response to suffering and to bad things happening is found among atheists or religious people who have their doubts. It is one biologist Jerry Coyne and others use to buttress their views that God does not exist. Coyne states,

> Our very world testifies constantly against God. Take natural selection, a process that is cruel, painful, and wasteful. After Darwin's

idea displaced Genesis-based Creationism, the theological sausage grinder designed to transform scientific necessities into religious virtues—rationalised why it was better for God to have used natural selection to produce human beings. Needless to say, that argument doesn't fit with an all-loving God. (www.newstatesman.com/religion/2011/07/god-evidence-believe-world)

I remember reading about someone who asked such a question and, consequently, took a completely different direction in life. The story was in Lee Strobel's book, *The Case for Faith: A Journalist Investigates the Toughest Objections to Christianity* (Grand Rapids MI: Zondervan, 2000), about Charles Templeton, a man who was a close friend and evangelistic colleague to Billy Graham. Templeton traveled the nation and world in the 1940s, preaching about the reality of God and God's love for everyone, communicating to thousands and leading countless numbers of people to turn to God and become followers of Jesus Christ. But everything changed after he saw one picture in a *Life* magazine. Strobel traveled to Canada to meet Templeton and learn more, carrying with him Templeton's book, *Farewell to God: My Reasons for Rejecting the Christian Faith* (Toronto: McClelland and Stewart, 1996). The interview, described by Strobel in *The Case for Faith*, shows Templeton's response to suffering as seen in the *Life* magazine picture:

> [Charles Templeton] narrowed his eyes a bit and looked off to the side, as if he were viewing the photo afresh and reliving the moment. "It was a picture of a black woman in Northern Africa," he explained. "They were experiencing a devastating drought. And she was holding her dead baby in her arms and looking up to heaven with the most forlorn expression. I looked at it and I thought, 'Is it possible to believe that there is a loving or caring Creator when all this woman needed was rain?'"
>
> As he emphasized the word rain, his bushy gray eyebrows shot up and his arms gestured toward heaven as if beckoning for a response. "How could a loving God do this to a woman . . . . Who runs the rain? I don't; you don't. He does—or that's what I thought." (13–14)

As revealed in this interview with Templeton toward the end of his life, he couldn't get this picture out of his mind and his heart, regardless of his well-conditioned responses to skeptic's questions. As he looked at the cover, his "why" question for God ultimately led him to reason that the only answer was that there was no God to answer, for no God of love would ever allow a child or its mother to suffer and die like that. There is no evidence that Templeton ever responded to suffering and pain in any other way than by rejecting his belief in God. Templeton's view, while found in someone going from evangelistic fervor to a complete rejection of God, is not an uncommon response to the question of why.

Bad Things Happen to Good People

I heard about another response to tragedy early in my ministry, taking special interest in it because my mother was in an ongoing battle for her life against a rare form of cancer. I found the response in the book *When Bad Things Happen to Good People* by Rabbi Harold Kushner (New York: Schocken Books, 1981). The title certainly got my attention as I couldn't help wondering why she had to suffer as she did. She was "good people" and as godly a woman as I knew. She had touched countless lives while teaching preschool, ministering to ninth grade girls, and leading Cub Scouts through the drill. As I watched her suffer through chemotherapy, radiation, and experimental treatments for nine years, I often wondered, "Why, God?" I couldn't help wondering why God would hinder someone who was contributing so much to his kingdom in this world. Here was the most selfless person I had ever known. Here was a woman who was busy serving her family (and God knew we needed that kind of attention!), her church, her high school girls' Sunday school class, her neighbors, her friends, and now her grandchildren. And bad things were happening to her, slowly taking her away from it all.

There is a long list of good people who have had bad things happen to them. It is staggering to consider the people who died in their prime, right at the point when it seemed they were making the greatest difference in the world. Images of the Holocaust, the words in the diary of Anne Frank, or the raw memories of Elie Wiesel remind us of people, so many of them young, whose good lives were snuffed out by an evil person. Bad things continue to happen to good people, and these events remain inexplicable.

Yes, There Is a God, But He Doesn't Get Involved

There is also the Deist response to suffering and tragedy. Deism holds that God is like a watchmaker, putting all the pieces together after creating them but then walking away from his creation, allowing it to run on its own until time runs out. Those with this view tend to explain suffering and tragedy as a part of life without God's involvement. Sure, God exists, but God isn't involved in stopping buses, curing cancer, redirecting hurricanes, mending hearts, or helping one find the right spouse.

Other Pastors

As we have walked through these days without our Maggie Lee, it has been helpful for me to turn to more positive responses. I have found it most encouraging to read about the experiences of two other pastors, John Claypool and William Sloane Coffin, who also lost their children. I had admired both pastors through the years, but I had not remembered that both had gone through the same kind of suffering I now knew. I read their writing in a whole new way, one that opened new avenues of healing for me. The first book, John Claypool's *Tracks of a Fellow Struggler* (1974; rev. ed., New Orleans: Insight Press, 1995), is a collection of Claypool's sermon responses to his young daughter's death from leukemia. He found that writing and preaching these sermons was therapeutic after he lost Laura Lue. Countless grievers ever since have found his words helpful as well, as indicated by the prevalence of his books on the bedside stands of the bereaved. We received copy after copy in the mail from friends and strangers, usually with a note about how helpful Claypool's words were for them in their own grief. They were helpful indeed.

It would be hard to condense Claypool's words and their impact in this chapter, but one thing he wrote reveals his responses to the questions we ask of God when we face tragedy. His book reveals not only his own questions and anguish but also those of other people.

Dr. Carlyle Marney, for example, wrote a letter to Claypool just before Laura Lue died. About that letter, Claypool wrote, "This is why I found such help in a letter I received from Dr. Carlyle Marney just before Laura Lue died. He admitted that he had no word for the suffering of the innocent and never had, but he said, 'fall back on the notion that God has a lot to give account for.'" (Kindle edition location [KL] 410)

Claypool also noted, "I do not believe God wants me to hold in these questions that burn in my heart and soul—questions like: 'Why is there Leukemia? Why are children of promise cut down at the age of ten? Why did you let Laura Lue suffer so excruciatingly and then let her die?' I am really honoring God when I come clean and say, 'You owe me an explanation'" (KL 415).

For years, I had found comfort and inspiration in Claypool's words, but when my own tragedy occurred, they helped me in a whole new way. If I had to point to just one thing I learned from Claypool's response to his daughter's death, it is to be grateful. Even while experiencing the frustration and helplessness of not understanding why God allowed Maggie Lee to die, I found something I could do: be thankful for the gift of her life. Claypool found that he had two alternatives: he could "dwell on the fact that she has been taken away, and dissolve in remorse that all of this is gone forever. Or, focusing on the wonder that she was ever given at all, I can resolve to be grateful that we shared life, even for an all-too-short ten years" (KL 477).

As I think about the incredible life Maggie Lee lived and shared, there is so much for which to be thankful. I am blessed by every minute of every one of our twelve years together.

William Sloane Coffin also helped me. Even though I had been aware of Coffin's work in civil rights and his pastorate at the famous Riverside Church in New York, I had not read his biography. I remembered something about his son's death, but I wasn't sure what had happened. I found a copy of *William Sloane Coffin, Jr.: A Holy Impatience*, by Warren Goldstein (New Haven: Yale University Press, 2004). Goldstein wrote of how Coffin's son, Alex, was in college, heading home from a night of celebration in 1983, when he lost control of his car and crashed into a seawall in South Boston Harbor. The passenger was able to escape, but Alex Coffin died in the cold waters that night. As Coffin heard the news, he was devastated. Two days later, Coffin performed the funeral for his son, something unimaginable for most any minister, but not for him. This was his way of dealing with the tragedy. One of Coffin's friends, Randy, recalled that he handled it publicly better than privately. Goldstein quotes him:

> "The mystery to me," Randy admitted, "is how anyone at a time like that could choose to handle [it] in that way as opposed to privately, quietly." The fact was that Coffin knew no other way to grapple with his own deepest emotions. For nearly thirty years he had addressed the most important things in his life by talking about them from a pulpit in front of a congregation. He was not given to long personal conversations about somber subjects. (KL 4711–12)

As I read these words, I could identify with Coffin. Preaching had been my therapy, allowing me to process alone and then aloud my hurts and struggles with the suffering and death of my mother and, two years later, my father-in-law. The practice of studying Scripture each week to prepare for sermons was essential to my soul's progress. The greatest irony for an introvert like me is that standing in front of a congregation every Sunday was the only way I could find help with my grief. I would often catch myself weeping, wondering if I was turning into a Jim Baker or Jimmy Swaggart with my uncontrollable tear ducts. As I look back, God was speaking just as much into me as I was counting on him to speak through me. Reading about Coffin reminded me again of the acceptability of such homiletical therapy.

Coffin's own words from his funeral sermon for his son reminded me of the ridiculous notion referred to above—one that some people believe though rarely say out loud—that God is angry and caused a death to punish the person or to teach a lesson. As quoted by Goldstein, Coffin

> confessed that "nothing so infuriates me as the incapacity of seemingly intelligent people to get it through their heads that God doesn't go around this world with his finger on triggers, his fist around knives, his hands on steering wheels." Quite the contrary:

"My own consolation lies in knowing that it was not the will of God that Alex die; that when the waves closed over the sinking car, God's heart was the first of all our hearts to break."[KL 4724]

"God's heart was the first of all our hearts to break." Now that is a phrase representing the merciful consolation of God for the overwhelming needs of humankind. That is a phrase whose truth is best observed in the self-emptying of God in the Bethlehem manger, the streets of Galilee, the Sermon on the Mount, the tears at Lazarus's grave, the upper room, the cross of Calvary, and the empty tomb. As I thought about Maggie Lee being tossed and thrown forcefully and helplessly, ending up trapped under the weight of the bus, I could know that God's heart was breaking as it had happened. This still doesn't answer the question of "why," but I have come to a place of acceptance that this question will have no answer. Continuing to pursue the question with that realization would have no value for me and would probably lead to a life of bitterness and unhealthy grief. Knowing there is no answer I can understand this side of heaven and knowing that Maggie Lee would not want me to spend my life on such a pursuit, I have resigned to live with the question of "why."

Question 2: Where Was God?

Along with "Why did God allow this?" I have asked another question: "Where was God?" This inquiry has proved faithful as, in reflection, I have found not one answer but many.

This question stuck in my mind and soul within minutes of arriving at Batson Children's Hospital in Jackson, Mississippi, when Maggie Lee was first injured. I continued to ask it for weeks and months after she died. Though less frequently and with more urgency, the question still comes up on unpredictable days when the memories roll in like waves, creating a smile from joy once experienced but leaving pain from a loss now realized.

Asking God where he was is not a new question. A look through the Bible provides us with example after example of people who had the same question and who directed this inquiry to God both directly and indirectly, both with anger and with acceptance. The book of Psalms is a good place to start, as it is full of a wide range of poetic emotion about God and God's whereabouts in the circumstances of people's lives.

Psalm 10:1 is a great example of someone pitching a question of "where were you?" to God: "Why, O Lord, do you stand far off? Why do you hide yourself in times of trouble?" (NRSV)

This question for God isn't always driven by anger at God, although it is at times; mostly, it is on a philosophical and theological level. If God is really God, really omnipresent, sovereign, and loving, then where was God when this happened? Where was God when the tires went out on the bus? Where was God when the bus began to sway from lane to lane? Where was God when the bus jolted to a stop, rolling over and over? Where was God when the children were screaming as they were jostled from their seats, as they were thrown around the bus and from the bus? Where was God when this bus was designed? Where was God when the decisions were made to approve it and put it on the road? Where was God when the decision was made not to purchase seatbelts?

Christians finish Holy Week each year with the last words of Jesus as he hung on the cross: "When it was noon, darkness came over the whole land until three in the afternoon. At three o'clock Jesus cried out with a loud voice, 'Eloi, Eloi, lema sabachthani?' which means, 'My God, my God, why have you forsaken me?'" (Mark 15:33-34, NRSV). If my experience is typical, especially as a Protestant, we tend to read these words but skip their significance. We hear them but close our spiritual eyes to them, or we hear them and over-spiritualize them to detach from seeing up close and personal the humanity of Jesus. Jesus as Son of God, yes. Jesus as Son of God, suffering on the cross, not so easy to take. If we don't allow these words to enter us, we miss the significance of Jesus entering into our suffering and pain. To truly understand the presence of God in suffering, we must consider that God allowed Jesus to experience fully the agony of suffering. To understand our "why," we must take a closer look at the "why" Jesus spoke to God in his suffering. Jesus' question goes beyond "why" to "where." As religious fundamentalists torment Jesus and seek his end, as his follower Judas betrays his unconditional love and acceptance, as one of his closest friends and followers denies even knowing him, as he sweats blood in the Garden of Gethsemane, and as he looks down from the embarrassment of a Roman cross at his traumatized mother, perhaps Jesus is really wondering where God is as well.

Surely followers of Jesus who either heard about or witnessed the crucifixion of Jesus asked this question. One story in Luke's Gospel (24:13-35) is of the two individuals who were walking out of Jerusalem to Emmaus, escaping the horror of what had happened and asking questions about it. These disciples on the road to Emmaus, wondering where God was, found him in their midst. The resurrected Jesus entered into their conversation, and after a long stroll, he revealed his presence to them so that their hearts burned within them as a result. The irony is that God was with them all along, even as they asked questions, guiding them with the self-revelation of the reality of his eternal love, experienced tangibly in the breaking of bread.

The story of Jairus in the Gospel of Mark (5:21-43) is another account of people wondering where God, specifically God's healing power, was. I had preached a sermon about Jairus a few weeks before the bus accident. While sitting at the hospital, I remembered this man who had a young daughter and begged for Jesus to come and heal her. While on the way to see her, Jesus got diverted by another person in need of healing, only to find out afterward that it was too late for Jesus to do anything about Jairus's daughter. I can't help thinking that Jairus's impatience turned quickly to anger, taking the form of sharp questions for God that he directed at this Jesus who claimed to be God's representative. His daughter had already died. But Jesus said it was not so, becoming the punch line of the people's jokes and the object of their laughter. They obviously didn't believe God would show up in Jesus that day. God showed up, though, through the healing words and power of Jesus, bringing the young girl out of her "sleep" and back to life. I revisited the story of Jairus when my daughter was in need of healing, after I had been at the feet of Jesus begging for help. Things didn't turn out the same for me as they did for Jairus. I addressed this in the sermon I preached when I returned to ministry as associate pastor at First Baptist Church Shreveport. (See "Jairus Revisited" sermon.)

Paul's letter to the Roman church also deals with the "where" of God. The oft-quoted sentence, "We know that all things work together for good for those who love God, who are called according to his purpose" (Rom 8:28 NRSV), locates God in all things of life. Eugene Peterson's translation of this verse is helpful in understanding the impact: "He knows us far better than we know ourselves, knows our pregnant condition, and keeps us present before God. That's why we can be so sure that every detail in our lives of love for God is worked into something good" (*The Message*). This verse has been of help to me time and time again, as I think about the God good can bring out of something so bad. Whatever happens, even while we don't understand why it happens, it is possible to see God working for good. No event or death can trump God's power of redemption and life.

As I asked God my "where" questions in the midst of Maggie Lee's injuries and death—and even as I ask them now—I saw evidence of the presence of God. From the moment I received the news of the accident while getting ready to begin our worship service at 10:30 a.m. on Sunday, July 12, to the time of this writing, God has been with us. Though I couldn't see him physically or hear his voice audibly, I look back now and see that God was present in the people who surrounded the families of the students who were on the bus. God was present in the prayers that were lifted up immediately. God was in the offer of First Baptist members with jets to get us to Jackson and Meridian quickly. God was with John and Jenny Ugarte through the presence and words of two church members sitting with them in the Shreveport airport as they received word of their son's death. God was present in the ministers who met me at the hospital in Jackson, most of whom just happened to be in town for a youth conference. As I look back, God was right there with me as I heard for the first time that my daughter had a traumatic brain injury, something much worse than the broken leg or bones I assumed she received. God was present with me in the waiting room while a doctor and nurses kept coming in to give me updates on why they couldn't perform surgery right then—that one lung was blowing out, then another, and then her heart stopped three times. Even though it was a living hell in the moment, I can now see that God was there as Jinny was on her way from a conference in Florida, in the gut-wrenching stress of hearing the updates via phone and text, separated by miles and transportation obstacles from the bedside of her daughter. God was with me in a friend, Chuck Myers, a music minister there in Jackson whom I've known since my days of work at Camp Ridgecrest. He picked up Jinny from the airport and then sat with us as the neurologist met with us for the first time and delivered the news of the severity of Maggie Lee's injuries. Traumatic brain injury. Dangerous swelling. Bleeding in the brain. Cardiac arrests. All we could do was cry and pray.

I can also see that God was with us at the bedside of Maggie Lee for those three weeks that passed in slow motion and felt like eternity. As we looked at the laceration across Maggie Lee's precious head, as we saw the wires and monitors and devices connected to her, as we touched her swollen hands and feet, God was there. God was also with us through the loving support of family, friends, church members, and complete strangers. The PICU waiting room was almost constantly full of people who were there to support and the Murchison family as they waited beside their severely injured daughter, Lauren. God showed up in the rolls of vending machine coins given, in the bags of Cheetos, the bottles of water, and the clothes to get us beyond the overnight stay we had anticipated to the three weeks we were there. I found God in red beans and rice, a meal that a church group brought each week to the waiting room. That was the best meal I have ever had, consisting of pure love, pure God. God also arrived in the outpouring of love and help from the wonderful people of Jackson, Mississippi, as so many showed up with offers of meals and hotel rooms. One local realtor provided her home for a week, followed by the same kindness from the head of OB-GYN there at Batson. Chuck Poole, pastor of Northminster Baptist Church in Jackson, took us under his care, checking on us each day. Though I only knew him through his writing and his work with the Cooperative Baptist Fellowship, I quickly got to know him as his daily visits and phone calls provided me with comfort, wisdom, and strength. His quiet, constant presence provided a real ministry of Jesus' presence.

Knowing that God was with Maggie Lee all along gives me comfort as well. I have to believe that God was just as much with her—and even more so—as he was with us. Even though we couldn't hear her speak, see her open her eyes, or watch her breathe on her own, we believe that God was present with her, deep down, underneath the pain, the drugs, the seeming unconsciousness. I don't think I thought of it at the time, but the words of Paul to the suffering Christians in Rome ring true: "For I am convinced that neither death, nor life, nor angels, nor rulers, nor things present, nor things to come, nor powers, nor height, nor depth, nor anything else in all creation, will be able to separate us from the love of God in Christ Jesus our Lord" (Rom 8:38-39, NRSV). I had used these words countless times as a pastor and as a hospice chaplain, comforting those who were dying as well as those who were in mourning. They are words that I've used in my funeral liturgies and as a reminder to the bereaved family when they see the casket of their loved one for the last time before it is lowered into the earth. These words, however common and well used, were fresh before my eyes when my child suffered and died, instilling within me the comforting reality that there was no place Maggie Lee had been that God—and his love—was not present. God was just as present with her in the bus as he was when she was thrown out of the bus, as she hit the ground along I-20, and as the bus landed on top of her. Even in the midst of all of that, in what should have never happened, I believe nothing was separating Maggie Lee from the direct care of God's love.

Some of that direct care came from the hands of the Alabama National Guard, who just happened to be behind the bus and witnessed the accident. It is no coincidence that they were there, having been involved in training for battlefield triage and trauma that same weekend. They were immediately able to respond, stepping into the chaos of the scene. We learned about this while in Jackson, hearing of the soldiers who lifted the bus off of Maggie Lee and Lauren. God was there, wearing camouflage.

Friends and family showed up and saw us through the three weeks in Jackson. Parents, aunts, cousins, siblings, neighbors, and friends came as soon as they could, taking time off from work and family to be there with us. There is nothing more comforting in a time of need than seeing the faces of friends and family. Jinny's group of friends, who came to be known as the "Steel Magnolias," stayed for days at a time. Knowing that a waiting room was no fun for our son Jack, his friend's parents would drive over to Jackson from Shreveport to take him out to the movies, to the park, or to go swimming. One of our friends from Trophy Club, Texas, provided Jack with an iTouch, a gift from her son, who was about to buy it for himself but wanted to give it to Jack to have while he spent day after day in the waiting room. The Mississippi Cooperative Baptist Fellowship coordinator bought a PlayStation 3 for Jack to use in the long hours of waiting. In addition, the Louisiana and Arkansas state coordinators of Cooperative Baptist Fellowship as well as the Disaster Relief director arrived with prayers and an offer of "whatever you need." Dr. Greg Hunt, pastor of First Baptist Church during that time, made visits, even delivering our car and other items from Shreveport. Our First Baptist Church family organized things back home as the days passed, keeping our dogs, watering our yard, cleaning out our refrigerator, fixing our air conditioner, and keeping up with our mail. God provided his real and abiding presence through these friends and family, all in ways we will never forget.

God was there with our ten-year-old Jack as his world was shaken with the news of Maggie Lee's injuries. He was with me in church when we heard what had happened. He was there when we met with the neurologist for the first time. He was there at Maggie Lee's bedside. He was there, riding the seemingly endless, ever-twisting roller coaster. He was there when it came to an end. Jack was fervent in his prayers, patient in the waiting, relentless in his hope. And God was there with him.

There are many other answers to where God was at the wreck and since then. The list of how God has been present goes on and on. The rest of the chapters in this book are an attempt to capture most of

God's appearances, though the fact that they still continue makes our list incomplete.

So God did not pull out an eleventh-hour miracle. He allowed our beloved child to die. He did not swoop in and make up for the poor choices made by human beings along the way: those who engineered the bus, selected a cheaper-grade glass for the windows, manufactured the tires, or thought seatbelts were unnecessary. But does God still do the miraculous? Yes, every day.

Chapter 8

Welcome to the Club

In the three seconds it took to read a text message about a flipped bus, my life was changed forever. When John stepped into the pulpit on July 12, 2009, he received the message and likewise was never the same. The accident and subsequent loss of our child initiated us into a club of which we wanted no part: the profound tragedy club. Time wounds all heels, and now it seemed to be our time.

With lavish generosity we were welcomed into this fellowship by other members who knew what it was like to face the forcible amputation of a loved one and survive. That a person could even survive the experience was both encouraging and terrifying to me. Many times I longed to be in Paradise where there are no more tears, rather than here on earth trying to quell the river of mucous flowing from my nose. And from the letters I read, even from those precious people who lost loved ones decades ago, I learned that the pain would remain until the day I reach that Paradise.

From far-flung places, people wrote to us with a gentle word, prefacing that word with a snippet of their own story. So many of them began similarly: "You don't know me, but in 1983 we lost our son in a tragic car accident." Or "My husband was going on a business trip and was broadsided by a drunk driver." Or "My older sister died of leukemia, and I grew up convinced that God had taken the wrong child in our family." From that introduction flowed words of wisdom about God's sustaining grace and what their life was like now.

Author (and one of my favorite seminary professors) Calvin Miller says that humans have story-shaped minds, and that is why Jesus used parables to communicate what really mattered to God. Similarly, I have always listened to Jesus' stories as well as other people for clues about how God might work in my life. Faith is an abstract concept but immediately recognizable in someone else's life.

En route to our honeymoon, John and I took a puddle-jumper from Atlanta to St. Simons, Georgia. I spent the flight with my neck crooked around 180 degrees asking an older couple, the Yeomans, the secret to their happiness. Of course, John was mortified, but I got some great information. When we were blessed with children, I asked every minister's child who walked a path of faith what their folks did right or wrong. I have found that people love to tell their stories almost as much as I like to hear them.

When the bus disaster hit, I scoured the many books we were given for clues to surviving this situation. Of particular interest was how we could give Jack a happy childhood after the tragedy of losing his sister. It was something that he deserved, and we were going to try our best to make it happen. How do you assure your child that everything will be fine and that the rest of his family isn't going to die prematurely? You can't. All you can promise is that you will wear your seatbelt and get check-ups and take every measure possible to be safe.

I interviewed friends of mine who had lost siblings (I had no idea that many of them had gone through this until we lost Maggie Lee) and asked what their parents did right and also what they did wrong. As Jerry Sittser suggested in his book, *A Grace Disguised* (1996; rev. ed., Grand Rapids MI: Zondervan, 2004), we told Jack that this was a bad chapter in a really good book. We sought to put the event into a perspective that we by no means had a grip on ourselves.

We were grateful that other club members, both friends and authors, gave us clues to survival during the turbulent adjustment period when I regretted being left behind. A few common suggestions kept recurring: "Don't only treasure the child you have lost. Treasure the child you have left. Don't try to make the other child into the one you have lost. Talk freely about Maggie Lee. Talk about her virtues and vices and don't be afraid to express your sorrow."

I believed that all of those suggestions were valuable. Jack and Maggie Lee were so different that trying to force our son into her mold was never a thought for us. We laugh frequently about Maggie Lee losing her temper at the game of four square or her messy handwriting because all of those things made her the unique, beautiful, imperfect person she was. In our family, perfect never counted, but being able to laugh about your imperfections did.

As for expressing our sorrow, there was plenty of that. I believed there needed to come a point where Jack would have hope that I was still in there somewhere. It's enough to lose a sister; I did not want him thinking that he had lost his mother as well. A few months after Maggie Lee died, Jack (who had just turned eleven) and I were visiting her grave site in Tyler. On the trip over, I wept silently while the music was turned up. I adjusted the rear-view mirror to where Jack could not see my sunglasses-covered eyes. I prayed all the way down there that God would give me the strength not to cry in front of Jack when we reached the grave.

He asked me, "Mom, are you going to cry today at the cemetery?" with a worried look on his face. I had learned what a powerless feeling it is for a child to see his mother in pain and not be able to stop it. My mother is an incredibly strong woman whom I can hardly ever remember crying, so I had little experience to go on. I told Jack that I would probably cry, but that it was okay if I did. I did not want him to dread coming to the place where Maggie Lee is buried.

We arrived at Rosehill Cemetery on Broadway Street in Tyler, and Jack got Ellie the Chihuahua on her leash. I stared at the wilted floral cross arrangement over a bare patch of earth where my child's body was laid to rest and tried to absorb the insane reality of it all. Or, rather, I tried not to. God answered my prayer. I did not cry. During my newborn grief, my life was sustained with micro-miracles like that, and such strength carried me for the moment.

I often tell my son that I don't know how he feels because I do not know what it is like to lose a sibling. I cannot understand what it must have been like to drop off Maggie Lee at the church bus at 5:00 a.m., to hear announced from the pulpit that the bus had flipped, and then, while his father flew to Jackson, to ride in a car to Jackson so that another parent could have a seat on the plane. I marvel that Jack had the faith to quote Bible verses to me in the midst of such a terrifying situation.

I cannot imagine the strength it took for a ten-year-old to come in and pray for his sister, talk to her over beeps and monitors, and try to hug her over lines and tubes, surrounded by strangers. When Maggie Lee started kindergarten, he would stand and wail at the picture window, "Sissy!" because his best friend was going away. Now he had beheld her still body, spoken at her Celebration service, and placed a rose atop her casket.

My mind still swirls with the unjust reality of my child being snatched away at such a young age. Even though I have absolutely no doubt about where she is or how she is doing, I miss her like the part of my soul that she is—the extension of myself and, so much better, the friend who made even a trip to Big Lots a blast and the sharer of many an inside joke. I take comfort in knowing that she has entered her eternal rest; it just makes for a jarring reality for those of us who are left behind.

I approach every day with deep gratitude for my family as well as the saints who have walked in our shoes and who have reached out to encourage us in this journey. Some liken it to making it across a raging river and then going back to help someone else across. Although I have not by any means arrived, I have reached out to new inductees into the club because someone reached out to me in my total disorientation and let me borrow their faith until my own resumed.

It is validating to talk to someone who has been through what you are facing, whether it is divorce, bankruptcy, abuse, widowhood, or even losing a child. Mainly it validates your humanity when you feel completely lost. Certainly, you long for clarity on the unanswerable questions: "How long will I feel like someone beat me with a baseball bat?" "Will I ever feel joy again?" Just the anecdotal evidence that one day there could be a somewhat normal life awaiting me was the shred of hope that helped me survive.

Sittser's experience was profound: he lost his mother, wife, and daughter in one car accident. He speaks about moving from one person to another, doing CPR and trying to save the dying. Out of his experience emerged the book I have read four times in two years and taught in women's Sunday school at our church. The faithful steward-ship of his story is an inspiration to me.

The subtitle of his book is *How a Soul Can Grow through Loss*. Sittser writes in the preface,

> Sooner or later all people suffer loss, in little doses or big ones, sud-denly or over time, privately or in public settings. Loss is as much a part of normal life as birth, for as surely as we are born into this world we suffer loss before we leave it.

He leads through example, issuing the challenge that we are responsi-ble for how we react to our loss:

> It is not, therefore, the *experience* of loss that becomes the defining moment in our lives, for that is as inevitable as death, which is the last loss awaiting us all. It is how we *respond* to that loss that matters. That response will largely determine the quality, the direction, and impact of our lives.

The most important thing this book gave me in the first few weeks after Maggie Lee's death was a model of a Christian who had lost far more than I had yet survived and even had a good life because of the choices he made. Sittser's focus on the universality of loss was a good reminder that we were not the only ones in the world to lose some-thing precious to us. When grief is fresh, the temptation is to feel like no one has ever lost what you have. If nursed, this feeling can quickly fester into bitterness.

I knew that neither Maggie Lee nor the Lord would have me become a bitter person. I also knew, however, that the circumstances I faced were completely beyond my capacity to handle. I needed help to maneuver the minefield of loss. Counselor Linda was a skillful guide in this journey.

Two of my closest friends, ironically both named Gina, have their Master's degrees in counseling. In addition to them, many other friends and family members would have felt privileged to hear my deepest feelings, but I did not think it was fair to foist my radioactive sadness on them. Honestly, I felt badly even sharing the iceberg's tip of my personal despair with a paid professional.

My first counseling appointment with Linda began awkwardly. Because John and I had shared prayer requests so publicly on CaringBridge, she was intimately aware of our story. When I entered her office, an older man with exterminator gear was leaving. He tried to reenter the room a few minutes later until she reminded him he had already sprayed in that room. The office has high picture windows on the back and right walls.

As I began recounting our experience, I noticed in a large mirror the exterminator wandering past and then peering into the window directly above me. He repeated this as he rounded the corner and paused, waving a vigorous hello. While Linda tried in her most professional way to ignore the obvious, the comic in me called the moment, saying, "This feels like a *Saturday Night Live* skit." And we both chuckled. What a great gift laughter is.

A true gift that I will always treasure is Linda's affirming voice in my first season of sorrow. Even though I reserved my most devastated emotions for God alone, I felt unburdened when I was able to share the darker ones with her. It helped to have an objective ear, someone who had no agenda but to be God's encouragement to me. I eventually learned that Linda had lost a sister, so she had an informed perspective into what might help us rebuild our lives in a healthy, God-honoring way. She gave me permission to rant and rave when I felt like it and to feel the full weight of my loss, yet she applauded my desire to become better and emerge from it. She later told me how much she prayed before each session.

Among my bigger fears was that the profound pain would make me lose my mind. I remember driving to Dallas in December 2009. I saw a homeless-looking guy in rags riding his bike west on I-20 with a clear plastic sack of aluminum cans strapped on his back. The thought hit me that this could easily be me one day. I knew that I could snap and completely lose it. I had the strong desire to survive but no firm assurance that I would ever come out on the other side of this ugly sorrow.

God has been totally faithful in his presence and help in times of trouble; it is not his abilities I doubted but rather my own. I used to view myself as a moderately strong woman, but this loss revealed to me how tremendously frail I am. Now when I see a recovering addict or homeless person for whom life simply became too much, I suppose I understand just a little better.

I know that there is nothing inside of me save the presence of Jesus Christ that has kept me from plunging into total self-destruction. Losing my child has made me poor, disenfranchised, distraught, broken, needy, and desperate. That is why I relate to those in need. That is why other club members approached John and me with such humility: they know firsthand the stricken feeling of despair.

People asked me what it is like to lose a child. I cannot answer for anyone else, but the closest feeling I can compare it with, is that in-between feeling when someone else picks up your child from practice and she is supposed to be home but hasn't yet arrived. I heard that to be a mother is always to have your heart walking around outside of your chest. When your child dies, you know you will never see that heart again this side of heaven.

It's the same uneasy feeling a parent gets when out of touch with a child, the feeling that quickly resolves when the parent sees the child open a car door and walk up the driveway. Only in the tragic scenario, there is never the feeling of relief, never the feeling of resolution, never the happy ending of your front door opening and your child telling you about his or her day, which in Maggie Lee's case would be an animated story involving impersonations, gestures, and lots of humor. The wait for reunion is awkward, and you have to turn off your brain to it or you will waste the life you have left.

Because no matter what you experience, there are others who have been through it and survived. There are always examples that your loss is survivable. For those survivors who gently welcomed us into the fellowship, I am grateful. For all of the wisdom shared in passing, for the clues as to how God might sustain us and prevent us from being totally taken under, I am thankful. Not all suggestions were profound, but one proved to be an absolute lightning rod for God's creative redemption, something more than we could have ever imagined.

Maggie Lee's Destination Imagination Team from 4th grade at Lakeview Elementary (Susan Miller, Christian Conrad, Michael Tsapos, Clay Reiss, Diane Tsapos, Honor Fusselman, Samantha Miller, and Kristen Marxer) did a project as 7th graders titled "Music Heals the Brain." They researched the healing impact of music on pediatric brain injuries and raised money for iPods and CDs for patients. They won the highest honor at DI Global Finals. (Knoxville, TN, May 23, 2009)

Trinity Christian Academy's "Sonshine Girls" held a food drive benefitting 7 Loaves Food Pantry at St. Andrews. (Plano, TX, October 29, 2009)

Music teacher Betsy Jones and her triplets Will, Becca, and Hays, along with Annie Bell Clark Elementary School collected more than 2,000 cans of food for the Tift County Food Bank. (Tifton, GA, October 29, 2009)

Lakeview Elementary, where both Maggie Lee and Jack attended school before moving to Shreveport, held an entire Maggie Lee for Good *Week* including a canned food drive benefitting Roanoke Food Pantry. Kathy Carlisle generously had t-shirts made for the entire community. (Trophy Club, TX, October 29, 2009)

Jinny DeAcetis hosted a dessert party and requested that guests bring a toy for the local Toys for Tots campaign. Aunt Jinny poses with Marines and the generous donations of more than fifty toys for Chicagoland Tots. (Chicago, IL, October 29, 2009)

Terry Champion organized a balloon release to honor Maggie Lee.
Youth enclosed a note telling Maggie Lee's story. The Hensons were contacted by
one person who found a balloon and did a good deed. (Terry, MS, October 29, 2009)

The Jets football team collected canned goods for the Northwest Louisiana Food Bank. (Shreveport, LA, October 29, 2009)

Reagan Rees and classmates at Grace Academy in Dallas held a food drive for the North Dallas Food Pantry. (Dallas, TX, October 29, 2009)

Katie DeAcetis donated her ponytail to Locks of Love, which provides wigs for cancer patients. (Libertyville, IL, October 29, 2009)

Premier Imaging in Dallas held a "Koats for Kids" drive. They collected more than 500 coats at their different locations and donated them to Collin County Child Protective Services. (Plano, TX, October 29, 2009)

Cosse-Silmon Orthodontics collected candy to send to American troops serving overseas. For each pound of candy donated, patients earned a chance to win an iPad. (Shreveport, LA, October 29, 2010)

LSU Medical Center ICU nurses Michelle Bovenzi, Jessica Phares and Laura Briggs collected toiletry items to donate to the Shreveport/Bossier Rescue Mission. (Shreveport, LA, October 29, 2009)

Amy Peters, the California jeweler who designed pewter "For Good" necklaces, donated 100 percent of her online profits to Seeds of Hope International which digs water wells in Africa. (Photo on amypetersstudio.com Avila Beach, CA)

in The spirit of maggie lee commit To Do one act of kindness on OcTober 29Th

Maggie Lee's seventh grade class hosted a Maggie Lee for Good carnival at the 81st Early Childhood Education Center Street School. (Shreveport, LA, October 29, 2009)

Brianna and Ferrisa Childs in Early, Texas, along with Early High School's Fellowship of Christian Atheletes, collected stuffed animals for Toys for Tots. (Early, TX, October 29, 2009)

Colleen, Meredith, and Kathleen Doucet and Whitney, Delaney, and Andrea Pavell raised $5,000 for Cook's Children's Hospital through their lemonade stand. (Ft. Worth, TX, October 25, 2009)

Kellie Brisee and volunteers did an extreme makeover of an on-base thrift store whose profits go back into the military community. (Ramstein Air Force Base, Kaiserslautern, Germany, October 29, 2009)

Mandy, Emma, Zoe, and Ruby Post filled boxes for Operation Christmas Child. (Galway, Ireland, October 29, 2009)

Cousins Melanie, Bryce (front), Brinkley (back), Madeline, and Braden Richardson collect food for the St. Thomas More Food Pantry. (Houston, TX, October 29, 2011)

JoAnne McAllister at The Blue Cup Coffee House gave owner Kim Granum $30.00 in seed money to surprise customers with a free coffee. The cards she designed and printed had Maggie Lee's story, picture, and a challenge to perform a good deed that day. JoAnne's $30.00 multiplied many times over as patrons donated back to the fund. (Holmen, WI, October 29, 2009)

Jessica Diamond, a nurse who cared for Maggie Lee at Batson Children's Hospital, wrote an article about MLFG for the nursing school magazine, *The Murmur*. Pictured with her is Samantha Greenleaf who with father, Jay, brought lunch to the pediatric ICU nursing staff. (Jackson, MS, October 29, 2009)

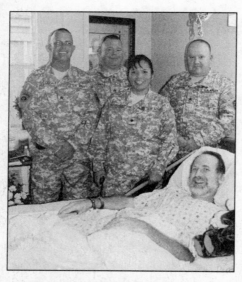

Youth sponsor and accident survivor Kyle Kelley is visited by some of the Alabama National Guard who gave emergency aid and amazingly lifted the bus off of Maggie Lee and Lauren. (Shreveport, LA, August 2009)

Cousin Judy DeAcetis gathers supplies to feed breakfast to the homeless on State Street.
(Chicago, IL, October 29, 2010)

Caddo Middle Magnet coaches Pat Hanish, Frank Wade, Glyndale McCullough, Suzanne Hughes, Linda Killen, and Julie Palczynski wear their MLFG Shirts. Profits from the shirts went to The American Heart Association. Tennis shoes were also collected to be recycled into a sports court. (Shreveport, LA, October 29, 2010)

Lisa Furnish decided to become a "Big Sister" through Denver Kids. She sent out an e-mail to her friends telling Maggie Lee's story and encouraging them to do a good deed. At the Denver Kids introductory meeting, three of Lisa's friends (who did not know each other) were asked to stand, introduce themselves, and tell why they were getting involved They shared that this was their Maggie Lee for Good Project. (Denver, CO, October 29, 2010)

John, Jinny, Jack, and Tom Henson with Mayor Cedric B. Glover's Proclamation outside city council chambers. (October 25, 2011)

Coach Trey Simmons and his Dodgers participated in the Shreveport Little League
"Maggie Lee for Good Classic Tournament" and canned food drive for
Noel Methodist Food Bank.(Shreveport, LA, Spring 2011)

Shreveport Mayor Cedric B. Glover models the 2011 MLFG T-shirt at a city council meeting
where he declared October 29th, 2011, "Maggie Lee for Good Day" and challenged
all residents to follow her example and do a good deed. (Shreveport, LA, October 25, 2011)

The First Baptist Church School cheerleaders raised more than $500 for Northwest Louisiana Brain Injury Support Groups with this snack stand. Pictured here are Caroline Rockett, Allison Grace Trawick, Anna Kate Geyer, Jack Henson, Madi Trudnack, Madison Atkinson, and Claire Barber. (Shreveport, LA, October 28, 2011)

In 2011, Chick-fil-A participated in MLFG for the second time. Pictured here is Jinny's brother's family: (L) Will, Kelly, Ted, Ben Richardson, John and Jack Jenson and (R) Jinny Henson, Judy, Blaine, and Ally Richardson (Bossier City, LA, October 29, 2011)

Katie Ashcraft and her mom, Lori, enjoy the Maggie Lee Henson Celebration of Caring.
Katie performed her original song, "Maggie Lee" at the Community Renewal Picnic.
(Shreveport, LA, April 16, 2011)

Students from St. Madeleine Sophie School in Bellevue were given slips of paper that read "One Day, One Deed, One Difference," on them They wrote their good deed on the slips and made a kindness chain that they presented at an All Saints Mass.(Bellevue, WA, October 28, 2011)

Chapter 9

Maggie Lee for Good

During Maggie Lee's Celebration of Life Service, our friend Marcie from Trophy Club, Texas, was moved by a song sung by Maggie Lee's voice coach, Leah. Leah sang "For Good" from the Broadway show, *Wicked,* which Marcie's family had just seen (Universal Classics Group, 2003).

We included the song because it was one Maggie Lee had sung throughout the house ever since she and John had seen *Wicked* in New York on her middle school trip. The thrust of the song was a sentiment we felt strongly: "Because I knew you, I have been changed for the better. I have been changed for *good.*" The musical, fundamentally the back story to *The Wizard of Oz*, is funny, vibrant, and redemptive, explaining that there is more to the wicked witch, Elphaba, than would appear at first blush.

Our friend Marcie was struck with a statement during Leah's song: "Maggie Lee . . . for Good." Later, she told me that it made sense given the positive impact Maggie Lee had on her family. She wrote it down on her funeral program, and a few weeks afterward she had rubber statement bracelets made and sent to me. Like many others who had written to us, God had used Maggie Lee's time in Jackson to move in Marcie spiritually as she was compelled to pray.

Kelli, a stranger from Texarkana, Texas, who had followed Maggie Lee's prayer requests from the beginning of the accident, e-mailed me in September with an idea. She said that with Maggie Lee's birthday coming up, she was going to remember our daughter by doing a good deed. She suggested that we try to get 1,300 people to do a good deed as well since Maggie Lee would have been thirteen years old on October 29. It sounded like a good idea to me; giving our hands and minds something positive to focus on was essential for that day. Having just opened the package with Marcie's bracelets, I already had the name of our little campaign: "Maggie Lee . . . for Good."

So many people had gotten involved in praying for Maggie Lee on CaringBridge that the power of human compassion paired with social media was obvious. The number of online inquiries about Maggie Lee was so large that it warranted a snopes.com entry, proving that Maggie Lee was not an urban legend. I figured that Facebook was a good place to start in publicizing our plan for her birthday. I created a Facebook group, and within a few minutes I had posted the link on my Facebook page as well as on Maggie Lee's CaringBridge page.

For all of us, the prospect of having anything at all to celebrate on October 29 seemed far-fetched. I did not know how I would live through my daughter's birthday without her any more than I knew how I would live through any other day without her. Still, I knew that a laser-sharp focus on my pain could be my ruination, while serving others could be my saving grace. We had no requirements to join, no structure, and no overhead. Spurred on by Maggie Lee's spark, the flame was lit.

I did the math of 1,300 people doing a good deed and figured that it would cover a few years of Maggie Lee's absence. Though she was not here, the thought of 1,300 people carrying her torch was redemptive. Mother Teresa's quote echoed in my heart: "Do not seek to do great things, but do little things with great love." Even if we fell short of the goal of 1,300 participants, at least many little things would be done with great love. I do not know exactly what those in heaven can see, but I hoped that maybe Maggie Lee would feel the splash of goodness echo up there.

When I woke up the next morning and checked Facebook, there were already more than 1,300 members of the group Maggie Lee for Good. What a happy shock that was. Simple in concept, open to everyone's interpretation, and contagious, the idea had obviously gained quick support. Immediately, we received messages from people eager to join, enlisting their schools and businesses in Maggie Lee for Good Day. What was so moving was how much thought people put into their projects.

Kelli suggested that since the goal of 1,300 was already met, we should set our sights on 13,000 people doing a good deed, and we did. By October 29, 2009, Maggie Lee for Good grew to more than 18,000 people who had joined through Facebook, the maggieleefor-good.org website, and CaringBridge. Just the thought that individuals, many of whom were strangers, would take the time to do a good deed to glorify God and honor Maggie Lee was incredible to us. Jeweler Amy Peters, touched by John's blog, designed a pewter charm that read "In Memory of Maggie Lee Henson" on one side and "For Good" on the other. She put Maggie Lee's picture and story on her website and sold the necklaces for $5.00, donating the proceeds to dig a water well in Africa.

Our friends Meg and Curtis, who work in printing, had made signs reading "Pray for Maggie Lee, Miracles Happen" during our time in Jackson. Now she offered to print "Maggie Lee for Good" signs at cost and mail them out. She needed a motto for the signs, and I thought "One Day, One Deed, One Difference" summed up what MLFG Day was all about. Signs soon popped up at the kids' school, in friends' yards, and even in yards of total strangers. Through witnessing people's response, I got the sense that perhaps our story was a small part of a much greater one that God was writing.

When we were in Jackson, so many times people's messages to us were about their children being touched to pray for Maggie Lee. We frequently heard from total strangers waking up in the middle of the night to check for updates on CaringBridge. It was as if our loss were a jarring wake-up call to people that life is short. Word about MLFG Day quickly spread to those in far-flung places who had prayed for a miracle for our child. The people who had prayed so passionately for a miracle of healing for Maggie Lee now funneled their faith into bringing good out of a disappointing loss. People were unwilling to give up on the idea that maybe there could be a miracle in the offing after all. If ever we needed a supernatural boost, it was certainly as we approached Maggie Lee's thirteenth birthday.

"One Day, One Deed, One Difference" 2009

Through a website launch (www.maggieleeforgood.org,), local TV coverage, newspaper articles, and Facebook buzz, more than 18,000 people worldwide committed to remember Maggie Lee in one good deed by October 29, 2009. In a University Medical Center article in which we were asked to explain the interest in Maggie Lee's story and people's overwhelming desire to participate, we said, "People have a deep desire to see good have the final say."

Maggie Lee for Good Day was a grassroots effort to carry on Maggie Lee's spunky brand of spirituality: loving people as Jesus would in fun and fabulous ways. Honestly, we were thrilled that so many thousands of people invested serious thought about what their project of kindness would entail. . . .

The FBC Shreveport Youth Group made cards and a care package to send to the family of Brandon Ugarte, who was also killed in the accident.

Practically every class from First Baptist Church School (preschool through eighth grade; Jack and Maggie both attended) had a MLFG Day project. Classes' events ranged from book drives for the Providence House, a donation drive for the Caddo Animal Shelter, a toy and book drive for the Shreveport/Bossier Rescue Mission, and the stuffing of Operation Christmas Child boxes. Also, Jack's class from FBCS performed stories from picture books for the younger children.

Allison and family in Shreveport created an info card to accompany treats that told Maggie Lee's story, explained that this random act of kindness was to celebrate Maggie Lee for Good Day, and invited recipients to join. They happily handed out the cards to friends, strangers, and the needy on October 29.

Linda in Shreveport printed MLFG T-shirts as a fundraiser for the American Heart Association. Our friend, Erin, a graphic designer whose father spoke at Maggie Lee's graveside, designed the logo.

Joe in Bossier City, Louisiana, wrote, "Funny how things come together. I just got done watching *Evan Almighty*. How do we change the WORLD? One Act of Random Kindness at a time. Maggie Lee, it's time to do the 'dance!!!!!' I got off work at 2 a.m., and I was wondering what I could do for MLFG Day. A coworker's battery was dead, so I helped him."

Penny in Bossier City wrote, "As we went through the Starbucks drive thru for my morning frappuccino, the cashier stated, 'The car in front of you paid for yours. It's Maggie Lee's birthday.' He then went on to say it was a chain reaction and had been happening all morning; so of course I paid the amount due for the car behind me. What an awesome start to the day! I was so glad that my son was a witness to the simple kindness of others. Thank you so much for sharing your beautiful daughter with the world."

Bryan, an ophthalmologist in Shreveport, performed sight-saving surgery on a young child free of charge.

Frieda, Suzy, and Judy gave a birthday party for the Cedar Grove Community Renewal Friendship House.

Josh got his school, Barrett Elementary, to collect pennies for the Providence House (a local program for women fleeing domestic abuse).

Kyle delivered three bags of food to the Northwest Louisiana Food Bank.

Keaton welcomed heroes home from war at the Dallas-Ft. Worth airport, while Reagan organized a canned-food drive for the North Texas Food Bank.

Jay and his daughter, Sam, took lunch to the ICU Nurses at Batson Hospital in Jackson, Mississippi.

Nicholas in Sam Rayburn, Texas, installed a hot-water heater in the home of a disabled man who had been taking a shower on his back porch. He never met Maggie Lee but learned about her online. He said, "If more spiritual leaders and political leaders stopped talking and practiced Maggie's lesson, the world would be filled with much more light."

Some people were moved by Maggie Lee's love for animals and donated to animal shelters. Angela from Tupelo sent this message: "I prayed for your precious daughter and rejoiced and sorrowed when she left you to return to her precious Lord and King. In her pictures, it is obvious she loved animals. Could we sponsor a drive for our local animal shelter through area churches on October 29? I would love to get this ball rolling if your family would be honored by this."

Mimi in Houston made treat bags for underprivileged kids, while Aunt Jinny collected Toys for Tots, and second cousins in Libertyville, Illinois, designed their own projects. Katie donated her hair to Locks of Love, while siblings Ben and Becky had a hot-chocolate exchange— a cup of hot cocoa in exchange for doing one good deed.

Cousins Madeline, Melanie, Brinkley, and Braden brought MLFG to the attention of their school in Houston. Maggie Lee's story was shared with the students, who were then encouraged to do a good deed. They then wrote their good deeds on cards, which were assembled into booklets and brought to the altar during mass. Cousins Will, Blaine, Ben, and Ally bought a Thanksgiving meal for a needy family.

Uncle Scott in Austin wrote about MLFG Day on his blog, and an attorney wrote back that he was taking on a client pro bono as his good deed.

Jana in Killeen was surprised to find out that her church bus did not have seatbelts and held a fundraiser to equip their bus with these life-saving devices.

K-LOVE radio (a nationally syndicated Christian station) ran an interview that spread the word even further. Long-lost friends from Waco, Texas, to Chicago, Illinois, found out about Maggie Lee's death and MLFG this way.

Whether through the catchy name Marcie came up with or the logo Erin donated her talent to create, yard signs from Meg or re-posts on Facebook from hundreds, Maggie Lee for Good was catching on. Weeks before October 29, 2009, we were asked if this would be an ongoing event. Certainly we would always celebrate Maggie Lee's birthday in this generous way.

Phoenix in Poulsbo, Washington, left this message on the Maggie Lee for Good web site: "In honor of Maggie Lee, I will be going to my local mall and my college campus with a sign that says Free Hugs on it and wear a shirt that I make that says 'Maggie Lee For Good' on one side and on the other 'One Day! One Deed! One Difference.'"

Cooperative Baptist Fellowship of Louisiana set up a scholarship for female ministry students in Maggie Lee's name, and Kyle and Charlene donated to that.

Our friend Cindy from Brownwood, Texas, had a sister Christine in Arizona who wanted to sell T-shirts and donate the profits to a charity of our choice. We chose Watering Malawi, an organization that Maggie Lee had learned about on our Youth 3G Weekend at Disney in January. Cindy's mother, JoAnn, made cards with Maggie Lee's story on them and spent October 29 buying people's coffee in Minnesota and encouraging them to do a good deed in return.

Rena from Tyler shared her project: "In your precious daughter's memory, I will make a donation of 440 holiday meals through East Texas Food Bank in Tyler, TX, on October 29. My thoughts and prayers continue to be with your family."

Kelly wrote, "It's a beautiful fall day in Cincinnati, Ohio. I always see the same homeless people on the same street corners when I go downtown, so today I brought them sack lunches and said, 'This is from me and Maggie Lee.' I made six lunches but I wish I had brought more—will continue doing this!"

Cathryn, who was Maggie Lee and Reagan's acting coach from the Summer Workshop in Dallas the month before the accident, encouraged her students to participate in MLFG Day as well and sent us this message: "I cannot imagine the pain that you and your family have gone through. But I wanted you to know what a joy Maggie Lee brought each day into my heart and class. She was indeed a special soul full of God's light and it shown everywhere around her. There are no words I can say to relieve your suffering but, for a moment, perhaps you can smile knowing all the lives that are better because Maggie Lee touched them and made them laugh and soar. I am one . . . as well as every child in her camp. All touched by such sweetness and spunk and positive joy. Sometimes angels live amongst us only for the time they are needed . . . and then they wait for us on the other side. All my prayers and love to you and your family."

Kent from New Jersey wrote, "I have signed up for MLFG on Facebook and will be honored to do something for her. Thank you again, and know that you have friends in NJ praying earnestly for you and your family."

After the accident, prayer requests spread and triggered emails from many different states and counties. Similarly, the grass-roots movement of Maggie Lee for Good Day was catching fire. Seldom in life does one get to witness the obvious movement of an invisible God on earth. What we were seeing unfold was as mysterious and unexplainable as a child dying on the way to church camp, only this time, it was mysterious in a good way.

Kathryn and Jason collected food and clothes from their students at Escuelo Campo Alegre in Venezuela.

Sara, an ex-patriot studying at The Sorbonne, handed out baguettes to the homeless in the shadow of the Eiffel Tower.

Kellie from Ramstein AFB, along with volunteers did an on-base thrift store makeover. The profits from the thrift store directly benefit the military community.

Sally and her family gave the money for a memorial water well in Haiti.

The Beloit *Daily News* reported a story about a man who walked into a local Taco Bell on October 29 and handed the manager $50 to buy tacos for customers. The man, who wished to remain anonymous, requested that the manager give each customer a note containing Maggie Lee's story. He had heard of Maggie Lee from an e-mail passed on from our friends or family and hoped that the people who received the free meals would commit their own random acts of kindness . . . and they did. By the end of the day, his $50 grew to nearly $500, which was used to give out free food throughout the day.

October 29 came and was celebrated in a beautiful way thanks to thousands of friends and strangers. I spent October 29, 2009, going from one local event to the next: from Broadmoor Lab's food drive to Cosse–Silmon Orthodontics' canned food drive to school to watch Jack's grade perform to the 81st Street Carnival put on by Maggie Lee's seventh-grade class. We were graciously given the gift of distraction by witnessing God's work in the world in a lavish way.

At the celebration party that night at church, posters were displayed of people's projects, from the "Lemon-Aid" Stand in Ft. Worth to eight-year-old Luke's smiling face and his quote, "I'm gonna give my body away when I die." This little boy committed to organ donation.

Friends came to the celebration party, wrote about their MLFG projects, dropped the papers in a bucket, hugged us, and ate cake. The rain came down outside and continued until the streets were flooded. We were eventually ushered into the basement because of a tornado watch. All in all, we were marooned at church with cake celebrating Maggie Lee's birthday. For good.

We continued to get thousands of reports of goodness that were done in Maggie Lee's honor on October 29, 2009. Non-profit agencies like World Vision, Compassion International, Buckner Shoes for Orphan Souls, Samaritan's Purse, Doctors without Borders, Locks of Love, organ donation services, blood banks, Heifer International, Watering Malawi, children's homes in four states, homeless shelters, food pantries, and animal shelters are just some of the myriad of organizations that benefited from Maggie Lee for Good Day.

All told, more than 18,000 people registered to be a part of One Day, One Deed, One Difference. Maggie Lee for Good Day evolved into a conduit of good will and positive energy, allowing people to redeem the terrible tragedy into something good. We surmised that those touched by Maggie Lee's story simply wanted good to have the last word and enthusiastically worked to make it so.

Chapter 10

A Table with Three Legs

Maggie Lee for Good Day was an event above and beyond anything our family could have done or even conceived of on our own. The prayers and kindness of others by no means went unnoticed, and the warmth lavished on our shattered souls cannot be overstated.

We proceeded that fall in our adjustment to being a family of three. I picked up pictures of MLFG Day, and the photo processor commented on a picture of John, Jack and me. "What a beautiful family!" she generously said, and her compliment took me aback. Staring blankly at the remaining members of our family and the gaping absence of our daughter, I finally said, "Oh, thank you so much."

I politely paid for my pictures and exited Walgreens as quickly as possible to get inside the protective shell of my car and weep. In reality, I did not even feel like we were a family anymore without Maggie Lee, and I wondered how anyone could mistake the three of us for an actual family. It was as if a hurricane had hit my house and wiped out the top floor, and then someone told me what a nice home I had, unaware of the entire second story that was missing. The problem is that in early grief, you can be mistaken for someone who still has both floors of your dilapidated soul.

Dick Stafford, a minister at Westbury Baptist Church where I grew up in Houston, lost his fourteen-year-old son, Andrew, when I was in college. Andrew and I had worked at summer day camp together, and he became my adopted little brother—whether or not he wanted to be. I adored Andrew; he was funny and going to have his own band one day: Mystic Rhythm. The fact that I remember his hypothetical band name twenty-five years later speaks to his impact on me. Months after Andrew died of a fluke heart malfunction, I asked

Dick how he was doing. He explained that in Hebrew culture, a grieving person wears black for a year as an outward sign of an inward situation, and perhaps we should adopt the same custom.

Christmas was approaching. A woman in our church, Carolyn, generously offered us her vacation home so that we could ski and have a change of scenery. We drove to Dallas and flew from there to Crested Butte, Colorado. Crested Butte has no sizable airport, so we had to take a shuttle from the airport in Gunnison, Colorado, to Crested Butte. When we arrived and I checked in to the shuttle service desk, the counter clerk asked if we were Henson, party of four. Her question cut through me like a knife. "No," I insisted, "there are only three of us." I specifically remembered making the reservation for three. Since I was required to give the name of each person as well as a birth date, I knew I could not have accidentally said four.

Insistent, the clerk questioned me again because their numbers had to add up. Again, I told her that there were only three Hensons. That settled, we loaded up in the shuttle bus and were ready to leave when another shuttle service worker ran out to the bus and said, "There should be four in the Henson party." John calmly explained once more that there were only three of us in the party. I stared out the window and quietly started crying. As it turned out, there was no "getting away" for Christmas.

The change of scenery was a welcomed relief, and although we sported our Burlington Coat Factory gear while everyone else in Crested Butte looked camera-ready for a Neiman's catalog shoot, we were grateful to have done something different for our first year without Maggie Lee. We often talked about how she would have hated being cold and how her dismounting the ski lift would have been a tragic scene to watch. My favorite moment of the trip was when Jack opened his gift of Taylor Swift concert tickets for the next May in Houston. Since we had met Taylor and her amazing mom, Andrea, the September before, he was excited to see her again. His wind-burned face beamed, and it made for a great picture.

Christmas was brutal without Maggie Lee, but it was made so much better than it could have been by the generosity of someone else who cared enough to offer us an experience we had never had as a family. It was a welcomed distraction that first challenging year, and we were touched. With enormous relief, we turned the calendar to 2010 and would be happy never to see the numbers 2, 0, 0, and 9 together again.

By January, the unpredictability of grief was getting incredibly irritating to me. I didn't want the world to know how sad I was; I just wanted to be invisible. I was uncomfortable with the deep sadness that flagrantly expressed itself without a hint of discretion. When you lose someone, you become a spectacle anyway.

Sitting in my car one day feeling like I'd been treated to a cement-truck mammogram, I shook myself by the emotional lapels and thought, "Jinny, surely you have plenty for which to be grateful." I began the ancient practice of counting my blessings, which by the way is super-cheap therapy. I knew that other people had gone through far worse experiences than I had, and I decided to make a list to see in black and white what remained rather than only what was taken from me.

I was always mindful that two people could live through similar experiences and have completely different outcomes. I knew that happiness was a choice that had precious little to do with circumstances. My normally optimistic soul, now anchored underwater, kept bobbing up to the surface to reach at least a gulp of the happiness to which I was accustomed. The struggle to the top seemed ridiculous. Every day I fought through the weight of my washed-out feeling in an attempt to break the surface and breathe in the joy.

"What I Know Six Months Out" is a journal entry on CaringBridge I began as an exercise in counting my blessings, as well as to record what I had learned in the six months since Maggie Lee's death. It was my attempt to glean the positive out of a situation whose pervasive sadness had worn me out.

CaringBridge

February 2, 2010

"What I Know Six Months Out"
I have often reassured myself in the six months since Maggie Lee's death that, although I have no idea what I will do without

her, I honestly didn't know what to do with her when she first arrived, either. Somehow this gives me room to breathe, and by the grace of God, I sense that I will adapt to my new life in some measure as I did before.

Of course, birthing a child and burying a child are two radically different prospects. On the one hand, you deliver a bundle of dreams wrapped in possibility and oozing potential and, conversely, in the other unnatural scenario, you lower those most treasured dreams into the ground . . . forever.

It is a disorienting experience, and frankly I am shocked to still wake up every morning. *A Broken Heart Still Beats: After Your Child Dies* (Center City MN: Hazelden, 1998) is the title of a grief book for parents and, alas, my heart still beats. I remember reading an e-mail two years ago from a friend whose four-year-old daughter had cancer. As I clicked out of the message, I sighed with relief that God had not laid that burden on me because he knew full well that I could never take anything so awful.

And then, in a moment, despite the diligent love that you have and the protective eye you naturally cast, a freak accident comes calling and is unaware that your family is supposed to be exempt. And as soon as you're told that your child will die, you begin to ratchet down expectations. You see a child in a wheelchair and breathe a hasty, "I'll take it," or one with a contracted little body but still able to communicate and think, "I would gladly spend my life taking care of her." But, alas, the ultimate bargain isn't yours to make.

I remember painting Maggie Lee's toenails crazy colors while she was comatose and massaging her legs when the nurses would let me take off the pressure cuffs. I told everyone that she always wanted to be famous and wouldn't she be irked that she slept right through it. I distinctly remember the kindness of Nurse Lindsay preparing her body for burial as it were by bathing her when the end was near, detaching the monitor from her head to wash her blood-matted hair so that I could braid it one final time. I also remember most of all longing to explain to them just who was lying in that bed covered with tubes and monitors, but that proved to be impossible.

It is still impossible, but the urge remains to remind the world that although she only had twelve years, Maggie Lee was truly a phenomenal little person.

I have learned a few things in my first six months of newborn grief. Certainly, many more lessons are to follow as I will contend with this ever-present absence as long as I shall live. I have learned that it is impossible to shake a good friend. Most people are lucky to have one true friend when it is all said and done. I have an embarrassing wealth of amazing friends and family who have shouldered the burden of loss with me. Souls, who have sincerely attempted to put themselves in our unenviable shoes, anticipate our needs and keep us supplied with books and Starbucks cards.

I have learned to treasure every imperfect day and the people who remain. Life is hard and will not for the vast majority of us ever turn out in the way we would choose. I guess that's why we're all so cranky. Since Maggie Lee's death, I have tried to suck the marrow out of life even more than I did before, enjoying my family as they are, not as they should be. We often unwrap the presents of the people around us with a conditional bent of dissatisfaction; we love our children but try to exact better performances from them. We appreciate our parents but our dad dresses funny and mom has a goatee. We are committed to our spouse but he sets the thermostat too low and she never remembers how we like our coffee. Losing someone I love has helped me to step back and be grateful for what and whom I have left.

Even though I was never much of a control freak, I now know that even the appearance of control over my circumstances is nothing but a facade. It is with infinite wisdom that the writer of Ecclesiastes compares our earthly existence to a fleeting vapor (Eccl 1:2). I have learned that even if life would have obediently followed my plans, that I would have at some juncture encountered a traumatic blow or two. Time wounds all heels, and many more graphically than mine—just consider Haiti. No purpose is served by prideful thinking that no one's loss can ever rival mine. If I wear my disaster like an orchid on Mother's Day, it will only serve to frighten people. Every human being will be confronted by unwanted circumstances that they can either accept or choose to wander down Main Street in a nightgown like Mary Todd Lincoln. As for myself, I never looked too hot in a nightie.

I have learned that T-shirt fronts serve as great Kleenex if you suddenly get an unexpected gusher. Gut-wrenching grief is sneaky and will typically ambush you at the most inappropriate moments such as in the carpool line, in Sunday school, or at the deli counter over cold cuts. Sometimes emotions are brought on by well-intentioned small talk such as, "How many children do you have?" or "Is he an only child?" I have found it best to answer the question as my life is now rather than to thrust my emotional baggage on an unsuspecting Wal-mart employee. People by and large are unprepared for the flood of toxic emotion a grieving person is capable of instantaneously producing.

I have learned that people do indeed want good to have the last word. When our three-week ordeal ended, over 250,000 visits had been made to Maggie Lee's CaringBridge site. On October 29, what would've been her thirteenth birthday, over 18,000 people signed up to do a good deed. On "Maggie Lee for Good Day," lawyers took on cases pro bono; an American handed out baguettes to the homeless French in the Eiffel Tower's shadow; and one man installed a hot-water heater for a disabled man in Texas who previously showered on his back porch. Schools had canned-food drives, friends had lemonade stands benefiting children's hospitals, and a pediatrician in Louisiana forgave the medical debt of a newly unemployed father, just to name a few. I have learned that when you are determined to wrest good out of tragedy, God and many other people will hustle to help you.

I have learned that although I struggle with God and miss my daughter desperately, I am not prepared to go it alone. I know intrinsically that God is the only path to true healing of which I can conceive. Although there are days when the searing pain wins over me, I have learned that my Heavenly Father is indeed close to the broken-hearted and that hope in Christ will sustain me until I see my precious child again.

I have learned that of all the things I have failed to prioritize, mothering is not one of them. Not that I was or will ever be perfect, but that I was dead-on in living with my family as my priority. I am devastated to have placed so much import on loving my children only to have had one of them die, but grateful that for a brief period of time I did what mattered most. When Maggie Lee told me that I was the best mother in the world, I would tell her that I was sure she would grow up and need counseling for something I had done or failed to do but that she would know that I loved her with all my heart. And she did. (—Jinny)

Writing became a healthy outlet for me, and people responded to me with experiences of their own. I devoured every book on grief that I could find. Books make excellent friends, and the inspiration in books like Gerald Sittser's *A Grace Disguised* (1996; rev. ed., Grand Rapids MI: Zondervan, 2004), the biblical books of Ecclesiastes and Job, Nicholas Wolterstorff's *Lament for a Son* (Grand Rapids MI: Eerdmans, 1987), and Elizabeth Edwards's *Resilience* (New York: Broadway Books, 2009) gave me inspiration and nourishment.

From talking with people who have gone through divorce, bankruptcy, infidelity, severe job disappointment, or abuse, I learned that the feeling of being turned completely inside out leaves your innards exposed and changes your life. It steals your sense of balance and changes your vision. When life turns you inside out, you notice different kinds of things.

CaringBridge

June 4, 2010

"Funny What You Notice"

Driving down the road today, I noticed a tacky roadside cross. It was adorned with an artificial dollar-store bouquet and had bicycle reflectors on each end, as if Lance Armstrong would genuflect were he into that sort of thing. And it grabbed me.

Here, memorialized in Sharpie and wood, was the accident site of someone's beloved. The makeshift monument hammered into the Louisiana soil was a message to the world that this spot is sacred ground not for what it gave, but rather for what it took. This place is where a parent's life was changed forever, perhaps, or where an orphan was born. I noticed this cross because now there is one hundreds of miles from here that unfortunately belongs to us.

I do not need to try to remember Maggie Lee. As Merwin says, "Your absence has gone through me / Like thread through a needle. / Everything I do is stitched with its color."

I think of her every time I hear the click of a seatbelt, knowing that a simple seatbelt would have spared us a life without her.

I turn on the radio, hear a song, and automatically calculate if the song was popular before or after July 12, 2009. If it was before, I perform a subconscious memory search of the way she would've sung that song or our conversations about it. This takes but a second.

I notice the bounce of a little girl's ponytail and search for Maggie Lee's radiant smile when I peruse group photos; it takes time to train yourself not to notice a face you've studied for twelve years. Just as you instinctively turn around when your name is called, you cannot help looking for the faces of those you love.

And on occasion, my search is rewarded with that face. I dreamed of her the night before last. There she stood, facing me at the top of the stairs, saying, "I'm ready to go," with her crazy morning hair and Nike shorts. I was actually a little embarrassed in the dream, embarrassed for thinking that she was dead when clearly she was alive, plain as day. "That was a weird dream," I thought in my dream as I looked at her full on in the flesh.

Unlearning someone's existence is just as impossible as unlearning your own name. You can't. So you notice. You still notice. Life goes on, and unless you want to petrify, you go on, too, as ludicrous as that thought seems. And when her favorite food or fashion items present themselves for notice, you gently remind them that you are no longer in the market for Chex Mix or rhinestone fuchsia flip flops, and they recede.

And a thousand times a day as life beats on, you notice. As you converse or see a picture or hear a giggle, you remember. And you are called to sew a new life.

In spring 2010, less than a year after Maggie Lee's death, we continued to sew our new life as best we could. We were approached by Community Renewal International, a Shreveport-based nonprofit organization. Community Renewal International (CR) was founded on the simple premise of strengthening communities through the involvement of neighbors sharing their lives with each other. Founder Mac McCarver was a go-getter who drove to Georgia to convince Habitat for Humanity founder Millard Fuller to build his first Fuller Center for Housing house in Shreveport.

Tom Watts of CR met with John and me and explained that the outpouring of kindness sparked by Maggie Lee's life and tragic death was exactly what CR was created to foster. Community Renewal honored that spirit by naming their annual picnic for Maggie Lee. The picnic, a celebration of all who cared in the community and certainly not only those on October 29, brought out people from all strata and ethnicities, homeless folks to jazz bands, and took place on a beautiful day.

Also that spring, John and I shared something significant: tutoring for the Lighthouse after-school program. We shared test-prep Tuesdays and Thursdays for a fourth grade girl. We enjoyed being in her world and felt increasingly convicted that this was what faith was all about. John had tutored the year before. In fact, Maggie Lee, Jack, and I had spent the first Friday afternoon of spring break 2009 helping with a party for the kids who had been involved in after-school sessions. The urgency to do something eternal with our earthly time gnawed at our souls.

Our afternoons in early 2010 were filled with Little League and Jack's shared lead in the school musical, *Under the Sea.* No singing was required, only a glut of memorized lines that were made easier by his talented choir teacher, Mrs. Alford. Jack finished his fifth grade year under the prayerful eye of his teacher Mrs. Ashcraft, the mother of Maggie Lee's friend, Katy. Mrs. Hadwin, another favorite of Maggie

Lee's because of her dry wit, was his other teacher. We all took in a collective deep breath to hold as summer approached.

Along with Jack's activities, an opportunity arose for me to perform comedy once more with Kenn Kington's Ultimate Comedy Theater in Pearland, Texas. Kenn has been a mentor for years, and his extending this invitation was both graceful and brave. He was amazing, and I was able to remember my bits and actually somewhat enjoy my time on stage. Friends Jen and Arnie came and, of course, my mother (probably in case I totally choked so that she could drive the getaway car for our hasty escape, which was thankfully unnecessary).

Three of Jack's friends from school were going to Camp Pine Cove, a Christian summer camp in Tyler, and since both he and Maggie Lee had been there before, he wanted to go again. After verifying that all camp vehicles had seatbelts, we registered him to go. As usual, I dropped off an embarrassing abundance of care packages and letters and was excited for him to be at camp.

John's father, "Dad Henson," who lives in Tyler, met us for Pine Cove's closing ceremonies. We had lunch and then stopped at Roseview Cemetery to visit Maggie Lee's grave under the big pine tree. It had been nine months, yet the grass had not taken root. Since we had four plots, one for each of us, we had chosen a large cross with "Henson" on it to head our little patches of earth. We decided to engrave Maggie Lee's picture on her footstone—the same picture of her and her dog Ellie that appears on so many of our publication pieces related to Maggie Lee for Good. Our daughter is happy and radiant in the photo, and it seems impossible that she is now buried beneath it.

As the anniversary of the accident approached, we decided to spend it in New Orleans for a change of pace. Although I had been to New Orleans many times, the beautiful architecture and history were still fascinating, as were the BP protestors we encountered along the way.

As we drove through New Orleans on July 12, right before the time of the actual accident a year before, we saw a large billboard with the name "St. Margaret" that featured a picture of a blond angel. We drove in silence except for the muffled crying we privately shared. We returned to Shreveport that day and attended a memorial service for the accident that was held in the new youth building at First Baptist Church.

In one sense, we felt victorious that we had all survived the year, but at the twelve-month mark the reality that Maggie Lee was never coming back could not be ignored. No longer did I expect to wake up at any moment and resume my old life, as I had a year earlier. While I had grown to accept the reality of loss, I honestly never stopped hoping for a different outcome. Even to this day, when I share Maggie Lee's story and describe her three weeks in Jackson, part of me roots for her and hopes that the story will end another way. That must sound ridiculous because I know full well how the story ends.

Summer drew to a close, which, as I have come to learn, every day and season will, whether good or bad. As much as we can dread holidays or anniversaries, the sun rises, we live the day, and then the sun sets and the moon comes out. No matter how fabulous or terrible, a day is only a twenty-four-hour chunk of time to be lived rather than feared. Whether this kind of thinking is sad or overly simplistic, it is the space in my brain where I file holidays. Each is merely a collection of twenty-four hours.

As fall began, our family began an exciting new ministry adventure: church planting. John resigned his position as associate pastor and with a few families, we started Church for the Highlands in Shreveport.

Another change was Jack's entering middle school. When he started sixth grade in August 2010, Counselor Marcie gave him the locker under the one that had been Maggie Lee's. It was strange to see her classmates in their natural environment without her. They were always tremendously sweet, but I never got used to her absence when I picked Jack up from school. When something irreplaceable is missing and always will be, you fight to minimize the feeling of loss even as you know it will forever be a companion. Time marches on, and you have to as well.

Considering the way time passes, I thought Maggie Lee for Good Day might have been a one-time event. Swept up in the fresh devastation of the accident, people supported it the first year, but I figured everyone might be too busy to notice it again. I knew that the second year of Maggie Lee for Good might just be my family and close friends remembering her generous spirit on October 29. Since I know God valued my little things done with love, I was okay with that.

In early October, we took a family trip to New York, where John and Maggie Lee had gone with her middle school group two years before. By the week's end, we had emptied a coupon book of all the significant tourist attractions. I loved the *Saturday Night Live* studio tour where my comedic inspiration, Gilda Radner, brought her "Roseanne Roseannadanna" to life. We saw the musical *Wicked*, whose song, "For Good," had meant so much to our family. I understood why Maggie Lee was more inspired than ever to be a performer after seeing that show on the Great White Way. I could envision Maggie Lee in her element at Times Square at midnight. One morning, we stood outside the *Today Show* with our "Maggie Lee for Good" signs and even snapped a picture of Al Roker, who graciously held one that I foisted upon him. What a good sport he is.

After our trip, there were just a few weeks before Maggie Lee for Good Day 2010. While I admire people who are inspired to start foundations and parlay them into huge, successful forces in the non-profit world, I'm just not one of them. I had done little to prepare for a second round of good deeds. For the first year after losing Maggie Lee, I had been doing well to keep us all in clean underpants. The only thing I did was assemble a simple one-page email newsletter sharing a few of the incredible stories I had heard the year before. This was mainly a reminder of the good I did not want to forget myself. Little could I have imagined the phenomenal good that would happen the second year of Maggie Lee for Good Day.

Chapter 11

Overcoming

Maggie Lee for Good . . . The Sequel

There were a few unexpected and wonderful responses to the first Maggie Lee for Good Day that unfolded right before MLFG 2010. One of these miracles was an anonymous donation to Shreveport-Bossier Community Foundation. As we ramped up for MLFG 2010, I began receiving e-mails about plans of even more participants who registered through maggieleeforgood.org and the Facebook page. Obviously committed to the idea of spreading kindness, some people's plans developed from a single spontaneous deed of 2009 to well-orchestrated events. The FBCS cheerleaders held a bigger and better snack stand benefitting Northwest Louisiana Brain Injury Support Groups. They took it up a notch by moving the stand from a cheerleader's front yard to the FBCS campus—during carpool. The drive-through service was an enormous success.

Jessie Keener, who collected a wagon of canned goods in 2009, organized a costumed fun run in 2010, made T-shirts, and raised money for North Carolina Organ Donation Services.

The second MLFG Day included bumper stickers and a challenge to capture pictures of those stickers with major U. S. landmarks, and creative photographs flowed in. Pictures of the Maggie Lee for Good sticker with the Seattle Space Needle, the Statue of Liberty, the St. Louis Arch, Tex at the State Fair of Texas, State Street in Chicago, and many places in between gave us a beautiful visual of the spreading movement.

In Los Angeles, an actor friend from high school, Ray Ford, and photographer Erik Fisher took pictures of Maggie Lee's sticker in front of the Hollywood sign and next to famous handprints in front of Groman's Theater.

"One Day, One Deed, One Difference" 2010

We got the news in October that an anonymous donor had given the Community Foundation of Shreveport-Bossier a gift in the amount of ten thousand dollars in memory of Maggie Lee. The kicker was that the Maggie Lee for Good Fund was to be given to nonprofit agencies of our choosing. The donors had actually met Maggie Lee and were touched by her sweet spirit as well as by the Maggie Lee for Good Day the year before. They wanted in!

Stunned and grateful, we prayerfully set about determining projects near and far that would have the deepest impact on the world. A local elementary school's clothes closet was our first project. Most of the children who attended this school had no winter coat or even socks, so we stocked them with both. Taking socks through the wash-dry-fold cycle is the bane of my existence, so I cannot imagine going to a Laundromat with all of our things and coming out with any socks. It is understandable to me that people would end up without socks.

Reid Doster, coordinator of the Louisiana Cooperative Baptist Fellowship, had just come to speak at our new church plant, Church for the Highlands, in Shreveport about the Cooperative Baptist Fellowship's partnership with the Baptist General Convention of Texas, Conscience International, and the Fuller Center for Housing's work in Haiti. After the earthquake, the Haiti Housing Network began recycling rubble into brand-new homes. When Reid spoke about the tent-city living conditions, I wished in my heart that we could pay for a home to be built. Thanks to this generous donor, now we could.

Locally, orthodontists Chris Cosse and Jeff Silmon held the event "Candy for Camo," collecting Halloween candy to donate to deployed troops through Operation Gratitude. Each pound of candy donated earned one chance to win a new iPad. Nine hundred fifty pounds of candy as well as thank-you letters, toys, and stuffed animals went to our troops.

Dr. Cosse said this about the project: "The Maggie Lee for Good project is a perfect way to honor Maggie Lee and unite the community in a way that can only produce a wonderful outcome. Participating in Maggie Lee for Good was a no-brainer for us, and our patients obviously agreed. We literally ran out of room in the office to house all of the donations that were brought in. It was such a good feeling to see all of the good being worked in her name. We chose the candy donations for Operation Gratitude (a US military support group) first of all, because we had two staff members whose husbands were deployed, and secondly because it was a great excuse to get off-limits candy for braces out of our patients' hands! For every pound they brought in, they earned one entry into a drawing for a new iPad. It started off as a 'patient only' competition, but soon so many people wanted to get involved that we opened it up to the entire community. We sent over 900 pounds of candy, stuffed animals, signed banners, and handmade thank-you cards to the soldiers."

Gina from Dallas explains why her daughter, Reagan, decided to do Maggie Lee for Good. "Why was my eleven-year-old so driven to organize a canned food drive at her school? I think it was a way for her to have control over a situation that left her feeling so helpless and so insecure about how she saw her world. When your best friend dies when you're in elementary school, it certainly doesn't make sense. Just a few weeks before Maggie Lee's accident, the girls discussed and day-dreamed endlessly about their future: living in an apartment together in New York City, working in musical theater together, being on Broadway and being famous in LA. I could picture Maggie Lee by my girl's side being her cheerleader. Maggie Lee was an unselfish encourager even at two years old. I don't think she had a jealous bone in her little body. I would often shake my head in amazement at what an unusual child Maggie Lee was. Reagan was able to channel her grief and somehow make purpose of a tragedy that made no sense to her. She and her classmates at Grace Academy in Dallas, through their food drive for the North Texas Food Bank, were able to change the lives of many families . . . for good."

Madeline and her mom, Aprile, in Shreveport brought personalized jack-o-lanterns filled with candy and toys to a class of special-education preschoolers. Says Maddie, "I participate in MLFG because Maggie was one of my best friends. Participating always puts a smile on my face, and I find this is a great way to honor how she lived."

Kandee paid for fifty students to wear jeans on Jeans Day at Youree Drive Middle School. She says of her small act of kindness, "It's the little things that make the difference. Sometimes something little can send one over the edge, and sometimes something little is what keeps one going."

Says Cousin Madeline in Houston, "Maggie Lee had a passion for life and was everyone's friend. She was always there to cheer someone up or give someone a helping hand when they needed it most. In participating in MLFG, I know that I am helping people just as Maggie Lee would have. I know that just by a small act of kindness, I am helping others and doing what my twin cousin would want me to do."

Though many projects were public, many more were simple, spontaneous, "pay-it-forward" acts of kindness. On October 29, Shreveporter Teri and her kids decided to buy someone a tank of gas. When they saw a stranded young family, Teri swiped her card and told the man to get some gas. Here are Teri's thoughts on Maggie Lee for Good:

> Throughout her life, Maggie Lee spread joy, happiness, compassion, and God's love to everyone she met. Her mission, her purpose, her legacy was to show each of us how to live this life. One full of God's grace, his mercy, and his love. And now, on her birthday, we had been given the opportunity to join others in spreading this message of love and kindness in her honor and in her memory. One day, my children and I made a list of all of the attributes that we had heard about regarding Maggie Lee. We wanted to figure out a perfect way to share Maggie Lee's legacy toward someone whom we felt needed her "touch."
>
> Here was our list: bubbly personality, winning spirit, compassionate soul, dreamer, expected good things, took up for the underdog, and ability to make everyone around her feel God's love through her spirit.

Okay, we thought, now what can we do?

The date was set. October 29. We understood the rules: Do something kind for anyone, for any reason and make sure that person knows you are doing this for Maggie Lee. Even if they didn't understand why we were doing it, we did . . . and that was enough for us.

It was incredible for us to imagine that we were bound together with countless others across this land with the same mission . . . to make sure we carried on Maggie Lee's legacy of love . . . of God's love. So the kids and I decided to fill up an unsuspecting and 'needy' person's tank of gas. "All the way! Fill 'er up!" We could hardly wait to say those words.

Our opportunity came by way of a young couple, their baby girl, and the hood of their car up . . . at the gas station. (If that's not God leading the way, I don't know what is!)

I walked over and said, "Are y'all having car trouble?" The young fellow said, "No ma'am. Just need a little gas to get home to my parents, but letting my engine cool off for a minute." I smiled and mentioned how very adorable their baby girl was. Then it happened, with one swift swipe of my card in his pump. (Oh! How very excited we all were!) This young man's eyes got wide, his mouth dropped, and he was obviously confused. I smiled and said, "Yes. Please get you some gas. It's for Maggie Lee."

He said, "I'm sorry? How much can I get?"

I said, "Fill 'er up! All the way. You have no idea how happy this makes us."

The man was in shock and thanked me over and over again, while his wife wiped her tears with her baby's blanket. If I had a blanket, I'd have used it myself. I couldn't contain the tears that were stinging my eyes. What a beautiful moment for my children to witness. Incredible moment! It felt so good. It just simply felt so good.

We've done things like that since, for Maggie Lee, but there is always something extra special about doing it on October 29 when we know that across the land countless of others are joining with us on that very special occasion marking the life and giving tribute to this one sweet soul by doing something good in her honor.

Maggie Lee "got it." She was able to unravel the "mystery." Somehow, at her tender young age, she was able to fully comprehend that the art of a warm smile, a tender touch, loving words, and a genuine heart for others was one way . . . well, the greatest way . . . to show God's love.

Here's the best part: Her story is not over. By our hand and through our mission to do 'good things' in Maggie Lee's honor and in her precious memory, we have the privilege of continuing her story and beautiful legacy of warmth, kindness, and love.

Moving Forward

After the overwhelming response to the second Maggie Lee for Good Day, the second set of holidays without Maggie Lee was a bit easier than the first. Turning the focus toward other people proved to be a great strategy for coping with the discomfort. For Thanksgiving Blessing, an event where churches, schools, and corporate entities donated food to feed five hundred people, we all packed boxes and then distributed them early Saturday morning before Thanksgiving. Being involved in ministry has saved me from a life of self-absorption, and for that I am eternally grateful.

Because we still trade off holidays, we spent Thanksgiving in Tyler with John's father, Tom; Tom's wife, Sherolyn; and Sherolyn's family at their country home with cows and horses and lots of dogs, a place Jack loves to be. For Christmas we returned to my childhood home in Houston, which was filled with cousins, one young enough to enjoy the pranks played by Jack's Christmas elf, "Holloway." It was great to watch Jack play basketball and football with his boy cousins. It's true that a mother is only as happy as her least happy child, and to see Jack enjoy the special treat of an extended family was all that I could ask for.

Before Christmas, I was asked to speak at a commemorative service for A Place that Warms the Heart, a grief support group in Shreveport. I prayerfully approached what I would begin to say to tender souls who have lost so much. I was overwhelmed by the task and prayed that God would give some shred of encouragement for their daunting journey. Written for the "Tree of Lights Service," here are my words:

Seventeen months ago, on her way to youth camp, my twelve-year-old daughter, Maggie Lee, suffered a traumatic brain injury when she was thrown from then pinned under the church bus in which she was riding to camp. Air-lifted to Jackson, Mississippi, she fought for her life for three weeks before being declared brain dead on August 2, 2009. Because she was such a generous soul, we allowed her to be an organ donor.

Though my story is dramatic, it is no more painful than yours. You have gathered here today to light a candle for your loved one who was taken from the earth too soon, whether a parent, child, spouse, or friend. Though our stories are unique, we share this in common: we are each left with a large hole in our souls that our loved one once occupied.

As we remember our loved ones, we are left with this cavernous, daunting impression they've left on our lives. There are many strategies to deal with these craters.

We can try to ignore them. Some people take down the pictures and try to bury the deep loss they have suffered, as if ignoring the loss will make the pain evaporate. Some attempt this erasure by turning a blind eye, but this is impossible. There is no suppressing the memory—it bubbles up subconsciously or is triggered by a sound, smell, or sight. Seemingly, behind every bush or commercial or song is our beloved's memory.

It is impossible to ignore the graphic pain that is there, a reminder that we grieve as deeply as we love, and that is why it hurts so badly. The fact that we lost such a vital part of our lives is the reason the hurt runs so deep. There is no denying the love we had, and even though the recipient of that love may have gone, our desire to express love for that lost soul never goes away.

We can try in vain on our own to fill the hole. We can attempt to replace the person with activity or dull the memory with alcohol, drugs, TV, hoarding, TV shows on hoarding, or other addictions. We can keep ourselves distracted in an attempt to postpone the difficult work of grief. But, as I have learned, there is no going around grief; one must go *through* it.

There are no shortcuts to becoming whole again after loss but rather the hard work of rehab to relearn life and try to function again. That is why you have chosen to be a part of this group; to gather with those who have had a similar loss and do the hard work of recovery together. This is a great decision given the temptation of filling the hole with entertaining distractions.

Quite frankly, it is a depressing thought to realize that your life will never be the same again, that in one instant everything can change. In a second, the paradigm of your life makes an irreparable shift, and the road that you were traveling on in blissful ignorance drops off into a ravine. It is no wonder, given how quickly the deep crater is created, that some people never recover from grief but escape into numbness to feel control in a world that makes no sense.

Another option of dealing with the crater is to focus only on the pain. We can succumb to the lie that no one else in the world has ever felt the pain we have and that no other person could have lost what we have lost along the way. In our vulnerable state of disequilibrium, which lasts for months and even years, we can tell ourselves things like, "How could my life be ruined this way? There is nothing left for me. God hates me and has taken away my best friend. Life will never be good again."

We can place all of our importance on this one loss and neglect what remains. The light switch is flipped off, and we can refuse ever to look on the bright side again. Some feel that if they were to live or laugh again, the person who was such a large part of their lives will vanish forever once the pain goes away. While the crater of loss is impossible to ignore, we cannot ignore the good that came before it or the good that could be even after it.

It is a damning decision to let your loss become your only identity, the only badge you choose to wear. Although I never met your loved one, I cannot believe that he or she would want this for you or the people who still need your love. As for my child, I know that she would have me try to live my life to the fullest possible; to be honest about the pain I feel but to trust that there is hope for tomorrow even if I can't feel it today.

What we tell ourselves about our loss will determine what we become from it. If we are brave enough to believe that there could be new possibilities out there for us, despite everything telling us that our best days are behind us, then there will be. If we are audacious enough to look beyond our craters to see the good things far in the distance, then they are possible. Conversely, if all we focus on is our crater, that is all we will ever see. The focus shuts out all possibility to see the good things far beyond what is in our line of vision today.

Psalm 34:18 says that God is close to the brokenhearted and helps those who are crushed in spirit. I can attest to this. Many mornings, I woke up shocked that my heart was still beating. Ultimately, I determined that since God left me here another day, there had to be a reason for it, and so I do my best to live.

We can acknowledge the ugly, uninvited, rotten hole and all that its presence signifies in our life. We can get angry and be disappointed because life has not turned out the way we expected it to be. We are not okay and will not be okay for a while perhaps, or maybe we will, but the only path to true healing is to feel our deep feelings of sadness and acknowledge our loss.

We have to feel the depths of sorrow and not ignore it by pushing it down or wishing it away to get better. And eventually, when we are better, we can honestly acknowledge that, too. We recognize the temptation to get stuck in our devastation forever because of the tragedy we have faced, but we also realize that we cannot be stuck and be better at the same time. The choice in large measure is in our hands.

There are places in our hearts that only time and God's Holy Spirit can heal. We realize that as long as we live, we will feel the loss, and that's okay. That's our reality now. We must realize that the hole we despise so deeply is a part of our lives, and we need to make friends with it. And, as you have done here in this group, make friends with those who have made friends with theirs as well, who are beautiful people formed from their craters and not just those handicapped by tragedy. . . .

This season, while we would gladly trade our problems for the former stresses of unwrapped gifts and overcooked turkeys, we are left with a crater and an extra place at the table. But also with the residual blessing of knowing that we have loved well and the provision of a loving God who knows all about filling in what is lost. And making us beautiful after all.

In January 2011, a bout with ulcerative colitis wreaked havoc with John. He was frighteningly ill, so much so that I was compelled to paint the stained spot on the living room ceiling in case things went south and the bereavement brigade started trickling in with casseroles. I knew it was bad when he asked me on Saturday to preach for him the next day. He always felt badly springing that on anyone else. Since I lead Bible studies and speak for church groups often, it wasn't a huge stretch, but I still found it a daunting task. Jack prepped the PowerPoint slides, I prayed there would not be any visitors, and thankfully we got through it.

Slowly, John got through his illness. I prayed that his sickness would be treatable, and it has been. The hardest part after sudden loss is waiting for the other shoe to drop. Once the unexpected happens, you never rule disaster out entirely. My friend Kandee gave me a key to her home with these instructions: "If the unthinkable ever happens, you are to clean my house before Grandmother gets there." We all need key-keeping, plan B people.

In March, Jack's school had its talent show. Jack and three of his sixth grade friends donned purple hoodies and "sang" a Justin Bieber song that mesmerized the second grade and under set. I even heard a kindergartener coo "dreamy" at the conclusion of the repetitive rendition.

Also at the talent show, Maggie Lee's friend, Katy Ashcraft, performed an original song, "Maggie Lee." Katy has the rare quality of intrinsic sweetness; she is a kind and beautiful Pollyanna. Katie was a precious friend to Maggie Lee, and the tribute she wrote was mature and somehow avoided the saccharine-sweet tone of so many tributes.

Here is her song:

"Maggie Lee," music and lyrics by Katie Ashcraft

I wanna tell you about a friend who was generous and kind
And she made a big difference in all of our lives
A heart of compassion that would help you any time
She defended the weak and stood up for what was right
She was a true friend to all
No matter how big, no matter how small
She made us smile,
She made us stronger,
And her love for Christ was greater than herself

She made us laugh,
She made us sweeter
Than we could ever be
Maggie Lee
Her heart, soul, and mind, she gave it all to Christ
Showing mercy and grace to everyone that was in need
A cheerful giver who had a passion for life
She always had a song to sing
And on heaven's stage she is a shining light
She was a true friend to all
No matter how big, no matter how small
She made us smile,
She made us stronger,
And her love for Christ was greater than herself
She made us laugh,
She made us sweeter
Than we could ever be,
Maggie Lee
Dream, fly, dance, sing,
Here's to you, Maggie Lee
Oh dream, fly, dance, sing
Here's to you, Maggie Lee
We love you for who you were, we love you for who you were,
Maggie Lee
We love you for who you were, we love you for who you were,
Maggie Lee
She made us smile,
She made us stronger,
And her love for Christ was greater than herself
She made us laugh,
She made us sweeter
Than we could ever be
Maggie Lee

In April 2011, Community Renewal's Maggie Lee Henson Celebration of Caring grew to a larger event, including an art contest for the two major school districts and participation by dance studios that brought in lots of children. Also new was the pet photo spot, which raised funds for the low-cost animal clinic, Robinson's Rescue. As we moved forward, more good was coming from Maggie Lee's brief life, but my recovery was taking far longer than I had expected or hoped.

That spring, I was in a grocery store where I rarely shop, and I flashed back to a summer day with the kids in their cover-ups going through the produce section of the store. The blunt baseball bat of sadness clocked me, and I immediately began to weep. I shot straight past the lettuce and cantaloupe for the rest room, my face immediately transformed into a scrunched-up faucet. I could not get there quickly enough to let out the gut-wrenching sob I was wrestling to subdue.

As I burst through the ladies' room, looking for a stall, I caught a glimpse of myself and was horrified. My face, contorted beyond Edvard Munch's *The Scream*, was pitiful. As I saw myself, I simultaneously pictured Maggie Lee's face, scowling and firmly saying the words "get over it." This waking dream of a reprimand stopped me in my tracks. Whether it was a divine visitation or my horror at seeing how ridiculous I looked and knowing what she would say to me, I will never know. The fact remains that Maggie Lee would not have me be a shrunken soul.

Spring events like the Shreveport Little League Maggie Lee for Good Classic raised much-needed canned goods for the strapped area food banks, and they raised our spirits as well. One team broke their huddle with the words, "Maggie Lee!"

Summer came, and we were blessed to be out of town on July 12, the anniversary of the accident. We were with my mother in Houston, who had surgery that day. Her twin, my Aunt Jinny, was there, and we had all kinds of fun with Mom as the anesthesia wore off. When we returned home on that day, a wonderful surprise awaited us.

When Maggie Lee was in second grade at Lakeview Elementary, I remember her rushing into my car at carpool line, bursting with excitement to share a story. Her eyes wide and her face dancing with animation, she exclaimed, "Listen to this, Mommy. This is *so* a God thing!" On the second anniversary of the bus wreck, something happened that was *so* a God thing.

My friend Colleen's Maggie Lee for Good project on October 29, 2010, was a family art show at their home. They raised $305.00 with this project and decided to donate the entire amount to our World Vision Child in East Khasi Hills, India. Amazingly, when we returned from our trip to Houston on July 12, we received a letter dated February 16, 2011, thanking us for the art show donation.

On October 29, 2010, Colleen and her girls had a MLFG Art Show. On July 12, 2011, their kindness boomeranged and fell into our laps at a most opportune time. And, without a doubt, that is *so* a God thing.

Here is the thank-you letter from our World Vision Child as she wrote it:

> Greeting from me and my family. Once again thank you very much for your love and your support to me and my family. I have received the gift you send me through World Vision. With this money we have spent school fees, school uniform, school bags, Gass Chulaspot [*sic*], text books, exercise book and trousercloth. These items are very useful for me and my brother and my sister. It has helped the burden of my father. We do not have anything to give you in return but only my gratefulness and gratitude and prayers for you. God bless you.

The timing of this letter could not have been better; Rinky's words were a reminder of the greater redemptive story God is writing in the world every day of the year, including our sadder ones.

I used to dread the twelfth and second of each month because of their significance. I do not dread them anymore, mainly because it is a full-time job to sustain that level of devastation. When your mind is fixated on dates on which you are supposed to be miserable, it is difficult to live at all, much less live in the present. God has encouraged me through the idea of overcoming I read about in the book of Revelation.

Since summer 2009 when Maggie Lee's life was cut short, I have become even more intrigued by the thought of heaven. Since Revelation offers a glimpse into heaven, I began reading it and absorbing what I read there about overcoming. Persecuted Christians in the first century obviously had even more to overcome than I do. Chastised for their beliefs, sometimes even to the point of martyrdom, their stress was excruciating and their grief intense. And yet they were called to overcome.

To overcome the loss of Maggie Lee, I have to make the decision to come *over*—to step over the loss. This doesn't mean that I leave her behind. She is always with me; we will always be together just like God is with me even though I can't see him. What I step over is the *loss*. Although the constant, intense grief has passed, it lurks beneath the surface and returns every so often. I must consciously leave behind the life that has already left me. I acknowledge that my Christmas card will never look the same, but I have a wonderful family even if there are just three of us.

I overcome because I know that a world with no tears awaits me. I do not have to fear anniversaries or dread holidays. My life is what it is. I can accept this change with grace or keep staring at the loss until I go insane. I will overcome because there is an eternal life for those who overcome, and that life starts *now*.

Overcoming is costly, but honestly, I can either overcome or become an obstacle for others to overcome. There are ramifications to not doing the hard work of overcoming, a price that we and those around us will pay. I am conscious of the ripple effect of my life and leery of causing more pain to those who have already been through so much.

We overcame the summer of Jack's twelfth year and were relieved to see the beginning of school. Seventh grade brought a new school, new friends, and fall baseball, which was new for us. And, for the third time, we reveled in the emotional high of Maggie Lee for Good. Since emails about projects came in steadily throughout the year, this time I knew that people besides our family were aware of and excited about Maggie Lee for Good.

Chapter 12

Proclaiming the "Good" News

While tutoring for the Volunteers of America Lighthouse Tutoring Program, John met Elizabeth Enochs and her daughters. Later, I met her at the annual Volunteers of America fundraiser, the Cherish the Children breakfast. Elizabeth is a sparkly person, lit from the inside.

From that brief encounter, a friendship blossomed. I met her husband, Lampton, and daughters and benefited from the gift of encouragement she gave. Another gift she and Lampton gave was bringing Maggie Lee for Good to Shreveport mayor Cedric B. Glover's attention. On October 25, 2011, Mayor Glover proclaimed October 29 "Maggie Lee for Good Day," encouraging everyone to do a good deed in her honor.

The city council meeting was full as Mayor Glover, in full-blown preacher's passion, delivered this introduction:

> We all want to know our purpose in life. There is tremendous value in being able to move around daily with a conviction that comes from having this sense of clarity.
>
> While we certainly can't understand why life can cast such dark shadows, it is still inspiring to know that it is not how long a person lives but indeed how well.
>
> I doubt many of the people in this room ever met Maggie Lee Henson. I can tell you truly it is our loss from what I learned about her.
>
> Maggie Lee was one of the most special people who not only understood her purpose in life but embraced it.
>
> Yes, I can tell you that she was a twelve-year-old girl with a vibrant spirit. I can tell you that she was a talented young girl with dreams of someday starring on Broadway. And yes, I can tell you

that she brought a special joy to her parents: the Reverend John and Jinny Henson.

But what Maggie Lee would want me to tell you more than anything is that she had a love for Jesus. A love that guided her life and the way that she interacted with others.

It was this love that made her the warm, caring soul that she was.

And it is this love that will keep her memory alive for many years yet to come.

Yes, losing Maggie Lee in that tragic bus accident in August of 2009 is a loss that few of us can fathom. But we're here today because the Hensons know that Maggie Lee understood her purpose, and that purpose was to touch the lives of others and serve them in ways that she could.

So I stand with them knowing that we can pay Maggie Lee no greater tribute than to make sure we celebrate this community of service and this commitment of service that she so well embraced.

And while it is only human nature for our hearts to be heavy when a life so young is taken, we should not forget that it is not how long a person lives but indeed how well.

And Maggie Lee Henson indeed lived well.

Those of you who do not remember, it was in August of 2009 when we lost several of our young people, one of which was Maggie Lee Henson. And referenced by my comments, her parents and those who love her are committed to carrying on her life and its legacy.

So it is with great honor and humility that I present this proclamation to her family and to those who love her in recognition of efforts they are carrying on.

Proclamation

Whereas, in the great unpredictability of life, tragedies occur, as did in the accident which cut short the life of 12-year-old Maggie Lee Henson of Shreveport, Louisiana; and

Whereas, inspired by Maggie Lee's spirit and commitment to help others, her family and friends have organized a special day of philanthropy and sharing to occur every year on her birthday, October 29th; and

Whereas, in the three years since the creation of Maggie Lee for Good Day, thousands of individuals and corporations have made significant contributions of time and money to the betterment of their fellow man; and

Whereas, in hopes to further inspire our fellow citizens to follow the wonderful example set forth by this extraordinary young woman;

Now therefore, I, Cedric B. Glover, Mayor of the city of Shreveport, do hereby proclaim Saturday, October 29th, 2011, as "Maggie Lee for Good Day" in the city of Shreveport, and urge all citizens to participate by doing one good deed in our city on that day.

In witness thereof, I have hereunto set my hand and caused the Seal of the City of Shreveport to be affixed.

Cedric B. Glover, Mayor

"One Day, One Deed, One Difference" 2011

Mayor Glover's proclamation truly set the tone for MLFG 2011. It garnered attention and exposure through KLOVE radio, Twitter, Facebook, Associated Baptist Press, and various other media outlets. Recognition from the mayor's office legitimized Maggie Lee for Good as a city-wide event—not just a few random family members and churches remembering a tragic loss. Unlike in 2011, where I had been the storyteller reporting what others had done, this year I wanted the voices of those who participated to be heard through newspapers and blog entries. We believed whole-heartedly in the life change that occurred when people's "do-gooding" senses were heightened and they joined with others across the world on Maggie Lee for Good Day. We wanted other people to tell their stories to inspire others with their creativity.

Threads of Love is a volunteer organization that meets a specific need by sewing bereavement sets for infants who die in the hospital so that parents may have something beautiful to put on their babies when the unthinkable happens. When a couple loses an infant, they are given a bonnet, dress, blanket, and prayer for healing. In 2011,

Brenda, who heads up the Shreveport/Bossier chapter of Threads of Love, wrote that 570 of these sets were donated to local hospitals for MLFG Day—more than had been donated in 2009 and 2010.

Peyton in Shreveport wrote,

Never had the pleasure of knowing Maggie Lee Henson. When she was in the hospital, I had friends describe her to me.

She seemed like my type of kid—smart, funny, outgoing, and passionate. Even though I didn't know her, or her family, I cried when I heard she was gone.

Fate is a funny thing. Some say it doesn't exist, that all things are predestined and planned. I occasionally agree with that!

I feel it was more than fate that led my son to play on a ball team with Jack Henson. It was an opportunity for me to get to know this awesome family, who Maggie Lee really was, and what Maggie Lee 4 Good really represented.

I remember the day I told my own sons why we were donating items, why we were collecting shoes, why I cried so hard when we did it.

We've always done charitable things, but this was different, I told them. This meant more because it was in *honor* of someone's child.

I explained it all to them. No one questioned my tears or frantic determination. They joyfully and willingly participated. They truly got it. When I helped a lady in front of me at Walmart who was $.53 short and was about to take the Dora pajamas out of her basket, the boys asked why I did it. I explained it was not only the Christian thing to do, but our ML4G deed.

"That day was last month, Mom," was the comment from one of the kids. It felt great to tell them, "No guys, that day is going to be every day." We will continue to honor Maggie Lee, not just once a year, but in all we do.

The DeAcetis clan in Libertyville, Illinois, each did something: Bill donated blood, Becky made hot chocolate for her soccer team in exchange for a good deed, Katie and Ben donated their own money to a charity of their choice, and Jody made dinner for a family in need.

Avery in San Angelo, Texas, presented MLFG to her school, Ambleside, whose fifth and sixth graders collected canned food for the Methodist Assistance Program and Food Pantry.

Katherine in Carracas wrote, "I wanted to share with you what our fifth graders did today for their Maggie Lee for Good project. A few weeks ago, we met together to talk about ML and what MLFG day is—and they brainstormed ideas they could do for our fifth grade project. This year they decided to lead games and activities for the younger kids at morning recess. The kids divided themselves into groups, thought up their own activities, procured the necessary PE equipment, and stayed in at several recesses to make signs and plan for today. Today they were so excited to play with the younger kids. The little ones loved it, and so did our fifth graders. I loved it, too, because more than any other service project our kids had come up with, this one most captured Maggie Lee's spirit to me."

Knowing that Maggie Lee for Good has blossomed, for so many people, from a once-yearly event to a new way of thinking has been incredibly uplifting. From Mimi (my mom, Judy Richardson): "Participating in ML4G these past couple of years has been quite a blessing in my life. Knowing how much she loved being with children, my deed that first year involved shopping for and assembling Halloween treat bags for children living at Greatwood, a shelter for abused women and their families. This year, I helped clean a home that provides after-school care to underprivileged children. Best of all is being a part of the yearly celebration where friends and family gather to share their stories of all the many wonderful things that have been done on this special day to honor the memory of our precious Maggie Lee."

From Camille Carlisle, Maggie Lee's friend from Trophy Club, Texas: "Since the death of my friend Maggie Lee, I have looked for ways to help people. I really did not do this when Maggie Lee was alive. ML4G has helped me grow up a little. October 29th is a gentle reminder to me of people that are less fortunate or in need. Participating in different projects, like the Lakeview DI team in collecting items and music for children with brain injuries, made me realize how blessed we are to be healthy. I could not help Maggie Lee, but I can help others through her spirit. Releasing balloons in Maggie Lee's honor in 2011 did two things for me. One, it reminded me that I should continue to do good things for people, especially those less fortunate, but it also gives me a sense of peace. Selfishly that is what I get out of doing things for others. I can think of Maggie Lee, talk about her, and feel peaceful because I feel connected still to Maggie Lee when I do things in her honor. I don't completely feel like she is not with me anymore. I can't really explain why I am not sad when I am doing things in her name. I miss Maggie Lee. I am sad when I think about her on other days, but October 29th is different. It allows me to take control of something. To do something. This makes me happy. She would be proud of her friends. We were proud of her."

Last night I had a beautiful dream about Maggie Lee. I was sitting down with her next to me with her head in my lap. Her eyes were sparkling and her voice excited as I patted her curly hair. I was so happy to be with her again, to have that missing piece of my soul returned. Fulfilling as it was, I knew in my dream that it was a temporary thing, evidence that the reality of our separation has fully sunk in, even to the depths of my subconscious.

I did not tell her that I missed her because I was so overwhelmed with being complete once more. I merely basked in our reunion.

"Mama, heaven is awesome. And Jesus, Jesus is *so awesome*! He's *so awesome*!" Maggie Lee spoke emphatically, and I could not get a word in edgewise without her interrupting. "Jesus is just *so awesome*!" She sat up with her eyes wide with urgency and excitedly conveyed this information to me over and over again.

I have to know that, of all the things she could have communicated to me, this was in fact the most vital thing. She was thrilled to be the one to share this secret with me. (She never was good at keeping secrets.)

In my dream, she did not ask me about anything on earth. All she could talk about was how incredible Jesus was. That was the point of everything—Jesus. She put her faith in him on earth but had fully experienced him in heaven.

Her life of faith proved to be a catalyst for other people's faith, and her tragic death on the way to serve others was an impetus for good deeds. So her life and death, above all, come back to Jesus.

And likewise, that is where we return—to Jesus, the clearest human representation of God. One who knows what it is like to suffer and lose but also one who redeemed the whole world because of the life that he willingly gave. Just when the disciples were the most devastated, Jesus returned with hands and feet of nail scars and a twinkle in his eye.

Just when we were beyond brokenhearted when our eleventh-hour miracle was denied and our daughter buried, he returned to our situation with a twinkle in his eye and redemption on his mind. Redemption of our darkest sadness into blessings in the lives of those in need in our world.

Food for the hungry, clothes for the naked, water for the dying, and encouragement for the disenfranchised. On October 29, Maggie Lee for Good Day.

While we will never fully get the hang of life without our precious daughter, we stand amazed at what God has done and what seems to have grown into a worldwide wave of kindness in her memory.

Jesus is so awesome indeed.

Discussion Questions

Chapter 1: "Mommy, Am I Going to Die?"
1. What is your biggest fear, and how has that shaped your relationships?
2. Can we ever truly assure our children that everything is going to be okay? Why or why not?
3. Who has been an example of kindness to you?
4. Maggie Lee had clear-cut goals. What goals do you have?
5. Who in your life lives with a clear purpose?

Chapter 2: July 12, 2009
1. How do you come to peace with the randomness of tragedy in the world?
2. Is God obligated to protect the innocent from the selfish and foolish choices of others?
3. Have you ever thought "God would never let that happen to me"?
4. Name a time in your life when your faith has been tested.
5. Do the most important people in your life know how much you treasure them?

Chapter 3: Week One
1. Maggie Lee's family was immediately joined by loved ones at Batson Children's Hospital. Who would be there for you in your darkest hour?
2. How would you balance grim medical news about a loved one with the notion that God alone decides our fate?
3. Have you ever prayed a specific prayer only to have the opposite happen? If so, did that change your thoughts on prayer?

4. When have you experienced caring firsthand?

5. Are you comfortable accepting help? Why or why not?

Chapter 4: Life in the PICU

1. John Henson writes about a ring given to Maggie Lee before she goes to camp. What is a special token that someone has given to you? What values does it inspire you to hold on to?

2. Encouragement is a powerful tool in relationships. Who is the most encouraging person in your life?

3. Do you agree that humor is an important gift from God? Why or why not?

4. How might God want to use you as a positive force no matter your vocation?

Chapter 5: Jairus and a Chihuahua

1. Do you believe that medical miracles still happen?

2. We will all face difficult medical decisions at some point in our lives. What is the most difficult decision (medical or otherwise) that you have ever had to make?

3. Do you think that organ donation is good stewardship? Why or why not?

4. Would you want your organs to be offered for donation? Does your family know this?

5. To what extent is our sense of control over our life false? What factors contribute to this false sense of control?

Chapter 6: Doodle Bugs in a Shoe Box

1. How did Christian faith affect this family's reaction to the tragedy? How has your faith shaped your daily actions and reactions?

2. Name someone who had an impact on you who is no longer on earth. What is the one gift this person gave to you?

3. What is the one thing for which you would like to be remembered?

4. Consider a disappointment you have experienced. To what extent has time mellowed that initial disappointment or devastation?

5. John and Jinny did not have the words to comfort the other John and Jenny who lost their son in the bus accident. Was this surprising? Why or why not?

Chapter 7: Questions for God: An Interlude

1. What has made you ask the question, "Why, God?"
2. Which of the explanations explored in this chapter have you heard in your lifetime? Did they help or hurt?
3. If you had an explanation for a hurt that God has allowed, would it be easier to take? Why or why not?
4. React to the phrase, "When grief is freshest, words should be fewest."
5. Do you believe God works miracles today? Why or why not?

Chapter 8: Welcome to the Club

1. Jinny quotes Gerald Sittser's philosophy that "We decided to view this as a really bad chapter in a really good book." Why is it easy to consider your present circumstances as a template for how your life will unfold?
2. How can God use your painful places to help others?
3. Who fills the role of wise counselor in your life?
4. How does loss humble us?

Chapter 9: Maggie Lee for Good

1. Why does tragedy sometimes bring out the best in the human spirit?
2. What was your favorite story from Maggie Lee for Good Day?
3. Is kindness really contagious? Why or why not?
4. What was the most difficult portion of this chapter?
5. Do you believe that God is the only true path to healing? Why or why not?

Chapter 10: A Table with Three Legs

1. What is the most difficult adjustment you have ever had to make, and how has God helped you with that change?

2. React to the statement, "I have learned to treasure every imperfect day and those who remain."

3. How does one begin to "sew a new life"?

Chapter 11: Overcoming

1. Why do you think people are compelled to participate in MLFG year after year?

2. What is one random act of kindness that has happened to you, and how did it make you feel?

3. To what degree does time soften the sting of loss?

4. Do you agree that you can either overcome or be a hindrance for other people to overcome?

5. Whom in our life—or in yours—would you call an "overcomer," and why?

Chapter 12: Proclaiming the "Good" News

1. Can one person's life truly affect the world for good?

2. What about this story inspires you the most?

3. What creative projects could your family, church, or school do for Maggie Lee for Good Day on October 29?

4. How were those who participated in MLFG changed?

5. In what ways has God redeemed the loss in our lives?

Afterword

The life and death of Maggie Lee Henson began a movement of kindness that is still reverberating. More than just a feel-good story, her story is proof that the human spirit will triumph even when the body fails, that people do want good to win, and that God is very much at work redeeming the world and even our worst-case scenarios.

The best way to join Maggie Lee for Good is through this Facebook page: facebook.com/MaggieLeeforGood. Click the "Like" button and you will be in the group.

If you would like to present "Maggie Lee for Good" to your school or service organization, go to http://maggieleeforgood.org and access free tools, graphics, and printables.

Appendix: "Jairus Revisited"

Sermon

"Jairus Revisited"
Mark 5:21-43
Delivered to FBC Shreveport on Sunday, August 23, 2009[1]
Crossings Contemporary Service

It is so good to be back with you, with my church family. It has been a long time since I have been up here, and so much has happened since I was last with you. I cherish the prayers, cards, tweets, notes, phone calls, and, yes, even the old-fashioned way of in-person, face-to-face communication. These have been a great encouragement to me and I know to Jinny and Jack as well. They have allowed me to know that you were there with me and are with me still. You have told me what has been in your prayers and on your mind during this time. I now want to share with you what is on my heart and mind today.

I was recently reading John Claypool's book *Tracks of a Fellow Struggler*, a book of his sermons relating to his journey with his daughter's struggle with acute leukemia and subsequent death. He describes his return to his congregation as "your burdened and broken brother, limping back into the family circle to tell you something of what I learned out there in the darkness." I ask your permission this morning and in the days ahead to allow me to share some of what I'm learning. I emphasize "learning" as I really am just at the beginning of this journey. I found during my mother's death, as well as after my father-in-law's death two years later, that one of the best ways for me to process my grief is through a sermon. The time involved in getting into Scripture allows it to get into me, to get into the marrow of my bones and into the substance of my soul. It allows me to express what can so easily stay bottled up inside of me. It helps me to share it with others, and it is my prayer that it may help you in your grief as well.

I wanted to start back today where I left off—with someone with whom I identified much during the three weeks we spent with Maggie Lee in the pediatric CCU at Batson Hospital. His name is Jairus, and he has a very limited yet greatly significant role to play in the Bible, especially as it related to my situation. I might as well have been on the dusty roads and with the crowds there on the "other side of the lake," at the synagogue where Jairus worked and met with God. I might as well had been there with Jairus, for he is someone I identified with and emulated each day as I found myself to be in his sandals, full of fear, anxiety, pleas, prayers, and faith in the only one who could do anything for my daughter. I wrote about this while there in the hospital and would like to revisit this story and look at it in light of everything that happened since then. I still think I am like Jairus, and I want to share with you ways that I still identify with him and his emotions here in this account from Mark's Gospel, but now in different ways.

The part of Jairus I most quickly identified with was his plea. I started to plea in this way at the moment I first heard about Maggie Lee's injuries. In that kind of moment, you don't just lift up a rote prayer or an elaborate oration. No, you cry out. And that's what I did that day, and it continued through the days and nights of our time there with Maggie Lee. My mind took me back to Jairus, for I had just covered this passage as a part of our Scripture on a Sunday not long before July 12. Jairus's plea was fresh on my mind, and it was of great help to me: "My little daughter is dying. Please come and put your hands on her so that she will be healed and live." Scripture was alive and real to me, for here was a dad in the same kind of situation. I could easily identify with his sense of helplessness, his raw fear, his abandonment of all else in the world, his consideration of Jesus as the only answer for his need, and his posture at the feet of Jesus.

I cried out to Jesus, fully realizing that this was something I could not fix. I am sure that Jairus, who was in a high position in the synagogue, had been able to fix a few things in his time. I am sure that he, like any dad, was one who had stepped in time and time again to fix a problem for his daughter. Maybe it was a fear she had when she was little, when he would come in and sit with her to frighten away any bad monsters. Or perhaps it was taking a broken doll and making it whole. I can even imagine him helping her fix a relationship with a friend when she was a little older, dispensing some fatherly wisdom to remind her how beautiful she was. I know all of this, for there were many times I was there to fix whatever problem Maggie Lee had. But this one was way out of my control, and I realized this in the first couple of days. There was nothing I could do. Nothing but cry out for the help only God could provide—a real miracle.

But I could also identify with Jairus in another way. As I have reread the passage about him, I have reflected again on Mark's words, "So Jesus went with him." How significant to think that Jesus, God incarnate, paid attention to this dad, listened to his plea, and then actually went with him to his point of need. And how important to think that Jesus went with me to the bedside of my daughter. As I look back on those dark, dreadful days and nights, I can't remember thinking of a time I felt like Jesus left my side. How did I know?

His accompanying presence came in several ways. There, of course, is the way he described to his disciples that he would be with them—in the presence of the Spirit, the Comforter. Jesus wanted them to know that, while he was leaving them physically, he would not leave them as orphans; that he was sending to them God's Spirit, the Comforter. Even with my questions and impatience and fear, I found that I had a Comforter reminding me of the words and presence of Jesus.

Jesus also came with me through other people. He was with me in the plane supplied by Jeff and Tammy Lowe. He arrived on the scene in the words and hands of the many Baptist ministers present when Malcolm and I walked off the elevator after arriving at Batson. He was there in the hands and brains and instruments of the doctors and nurses who were caring for Maggie Lee. He made his presence known through the countless visitors from here as well as churches throughout Mississippi, people willing to just sit with us in the way of Christ.

As I reread the passage in light of everything that has happened, I can also identify with Jairus's impatience with Jesus in a different kind of way. Jairus wanted Jesus to get to his daughter right away and couldn't understand his delay. I certainly understood that feeling in the three weeks of delay. Jesus, why haven't you done anything yet? Are you waiting for something? Are you waiting for me to do something or for me to display just a little more faith? Is there some magical prayer I am to say? Are you wanting to teach a lesson here? And if so, I am so not in for a lesson right now. My patience was running thin, and it didn't matter to me that Jesus was involved in things I couldn't begin to understand.

Now that Maggie Lee has died, my urgency and plea is gone. As I mentioned earlier, I do know that Jesus showed up with me and was right there with me at the bedside of my daughter who was dying, but the healing I desired did not happen. I am still in the place of wondering why; of not understanding. I do believe and am coming to trust that Jesus was up to something and that one day I will see it—just as Jairus later must have seen and understood what Jesus was doing with the sick woman he thought was a distraction there in the streets of his city.

This lack of understanding Jairus had was met with these words from Jesus, especially as the crowds around the two of them were questioning Jesus' ability to help: "Don't be afraid, just believe." As I deal with the inevitable emotional waves of grief, anger, doubt, frustration, and questions, I am resting more and more on these same words, "Don't be afraid, just believe." I now know how Jairus was afraid, and Jesus knows how I was and am afraid, and these words are for me today and they are for you as well. Jesus, the one who knows suffering and fear and death more than anyone and who has passed on to the other side—and with victory over it all—is perfectly capable and official to say these words to us. And we must receive them in these times of not understanding.

And, finally, as I read this passage again now, I realized that there is one difference. Actually, I didn't have to read it again to realize that things didn't turn out for me like they did for Jairus. He was able to see his daughter get up and talk. He was able to talk with her about